No Biting

No Biting

Policy and Practice
for Toddler Programs

Gretchen Kinnell
for Child Care Solutions

Second Edition

Redleaf Press
www.redleafpress.org
800-423-8309

Published by Redleaf Press
10 Yorkton Court
St. Paul, MN 55117
www.redleafpress.org

Second edition 2008
Cover design by David Swanson
Cover photograph by Gary Cook/Image Group
Interior typeset in Sabon and designed by Mayfly Design
Printed in the United States of America
15 14 13 12 11 10 09 08   1 2 3 4 5 6 7 8

Library of Congress Cataloging-in-Publication Data
Kinnell, Gretchen, 1950-
  No biting : policy and practice for toddler programs / Gretchen Kinnell. --
2nd ed.
      p. cm.
  ISBN 978-1-933653-56-3 (alk. paper)
  1. Toddlers--Development. 2. Toddlers--Psychology. 3. Children and violence. I. Title.
  HQ774.5.K56 2008
  649'.122--dc22

                                        2007036603

Printed on acid-free paper

To the teachers, caregivers,
and administrators who care
for and about toddlers every day

No Biting

Preface

The first edition of *No Biting* was the result of a task force formed to address biting. At the time, our organization was the Child Care Council of Onondaga County; in 2004 we changed our name to Child Care Solutions. For many years we had provided technical assistance to programs and advice to parents on an individual basis. We found that many programs approached biting by trial and error, trying a string of techniques in rapid succession in the hopes they might stumble across something that would work. The caregivers involved often confided that they were not at all prepared to deal effectively with biting. They didn't understand why the toddlers were biting or why the techniques, which often included punishments, didn't work. They felt even more unsure of what to do when biting continued and they faced what they referred to as "biting epidemics."

Many programs and providers we worked with felt pressured to expel children who were biting. Directors felt caught between the parents and the staff and sometimes between the parents of the child who was biting and the parents of the children being bitten. Parents called us with complaints of incompetent caregivers and unresponsive directors. Other parents called in anguish because their children were being "kicked out of day care," some before they had turned two. And the toddlers themselves were caught in the middle of struggling programs and angry parents.

As we wrestled with these calls, we wished there were written materials we could send to parents, programs, and providers. We found that while we could find many articles, they were usually short, too general, or limited to just one aspect of biting, and all of them could only offer a few suggestions for how to cope with it. Much of the advice that was available was questionable and ineffective, and some was downright cruel. What we were looking for was a comprehensive resource for programs that carefully considered all the issues related to biting in toddler care settings and contained appropriate, effective suggestions for everyone involved: caregivers, administrators, and parents. Since we couldn't find one, we decided to convene a group of experienced toddler caregivers and program administrators to do the thinking, consider the issues, and create the resource we had been looking for.

This group became the Task Force on Biting and consisted of eighteen caregivers and administrators from child care centers and Early Head Start programs in Syracuse and surrounding Onondaga County. Over the course of several months in 1998, the members of the task force met regularly and created a process to develop the resource. They began by identifying what they wanted it to address. At first, they thought they could simply gather the current information on biting, add some of their own thoughts and experiences, and organize it into a set of useful explanations of why toddlers bite and suggestions for how to stop it. What they found, however, was that they needed to go beyond simple explanations or solutions and grapple with the important issues at the heart of the biting dilemma: How do people look at biting? How do programs make decisions about their practices? How do programs deal with problem situations involving children? How do caregivers and programs respond to parents' concerns? How do programs respond to pressure from parents?

As the task force members worked through these issues, they realized that the discussions of the problems were as important as the resulting solutions. The Child Care Council decided to incorporate these discussions into a book so readers would understand the basis for the explanations, suggestions, strategies, and techniques.

Since the completion of the original task force's resource and the publication of the first edition of *No Biting*, Child Care Solutions has continued to work with programs, parents, and providers to address the dilemma of biting in child care programs serving toddlers. This second edition contains additional insights, information, suggestions, and sample observations that arose from helping child care programs tackle this important issue.

Members of the Task Force on Biting, Child Care Solutions

Jennifer Burns	CAZENOVIA CHILDREN'S HOUSE
Jackie Gower	CAZENOVIA CHILDREN'S HOUSE
Gretchen Kinnell	CHILD CARE COUNCIL OF ONONDAGA COUNTY
Sherry Knepp	KIDS UNLIMITED CHILD CARE CENTER
Linda Leone	CAZENOVIA CHILDREN'S HOUSE
Lynne Mathews	CHILDTIME CHILDREN'S CENTER 0042
Bev Meloon	SONSHINE CHILD CARE CENTER
Nancy Meunier	THE GROWING PLACE
Pat Nye	MARCELLUS PRESBYTERIAN CHILD CARE CENTER
Bonnie Phelps	CHILD CARE COUNCIL OF ONONDAGA COUNTY
Linda Ricks	EARLY HEAD START
Tania Scholder	SALVATION ARMY—CLINTON ST. DAY CARE
Bethany Scott	SONSHINE CHILD CARE CENTER
Carol Taylor	EARLY HEAD START

Acknowledgments

I would first like to acknowledge the commitment of the child care centers and especially the directors who sent their teachers and administrators to participate in the task force. It was their work that led to the first edition of *No Biting.*

I would like to thank AIDS Community Resources in Syracuse, New York, for supplying research data and information on HIV/AIDS.

I would like to thank Dr. Gary Johnson, associate professor of emergency medicine at University Hospital in Syracuse, for information on appropriate first aid for biting.

Finally, I thank the staff of Child Care Solutions for all the work they do to help child care programs and providers in our community work effectively with children and families and for their support of this book. I would like to especially recognize the people I work with every day on the education and training team at Child Care Solutions. Their work makes it possible for me to do this work.

Introduction

People who do not work with toddlers in groups might ask, "How can there be enough to say about biting to fill a book?" "Why would anyone need an entire book devoted to biting in toddler programs?" People who do work with toddlers in groups, and in all kinds of early childhood programs, however, never ask these questions. They know without a doubt that biting is a serious, complicated issue. They know because they struggle with it on a regular basis.

This was the opening paragraph of the first edition of *No Biting*. In the years since it was published in 2002, I have presented many workshops and some keynote addresses on biting. I have found that more and more people outside our field know that child care centers struggle with biting. They may not know exactly what the issues are, but they recognize biting as a problem. At a conference on biting held in New York, a local politician, Westchester County Executive Andrew J. Spano, was being honored for his support of infant and toddler care. After looking over the conference agenda, which included my keynote, he told me that he hadn't known biting was such a serious issue. He had an interesting question: "What do I need to know about biting as the county executive? It must be pretty important if there is a whole conference about it." He wasn't a parent of a toddler, nor did he work in a child care program as a caregiver or an administrator, but as the county executive, he knew he should be concerned.

The answer to his question was that toddler biting is quite common in child care programs, yet even experienced caregivers often find it difficult to deal with. Both parents and caregivers can become frustrated and angry, sometimes to the point that when they can't come up with a solution, a toddler may be expelled from child care. Parents who are embroiled in difficult biting situations at a center or child care home are likely to miss work—especially those who must find new child care. That means there are not only unhappy parents but also unhappy employers. Helping caregivers and administrators address biting more effectively with toddlers and their parents is important not just to child care programs and the families they serve but to the whole community.

At Child Care Solutions we have long been aware that biting is an ongoing and difficult issue in child care programs. We know this because we have more calls from programs, providers, and parents about biting than about any other issue. In our experience, no other single issue in programs for toddlers inflames parents and frustrates staff the way biting does. Of course parents don't want their children to be injured in any way by another toddler, but they are usually understanding and supportive of caregivers while they work to resolve problems like pinching, hitting, or even kicking. The reaction to biting, however, is usually different. Flesh torn by teeth seems so primal, so animalistic, and so frightening that it evokes very strong feelings in adults. There's still a little distance when children hit each other, but biting is up close and personal. We have seen adults completely lose control over biting—crying, cursing, even threatening staff or other parents. The most understanding and supportive parents can become exasperated when biting continues and nothing works to stop it.

Describing Biting

The members of the original task force found that the words they used to describe the problem of biting among toddlers shaped the way they thought about the issue. They needed to have a common understanding of biting and a common language to discuss the problem of biting in order to choose responses and develop policies. As a result, the task force struggled with how to describe or label biting. It certainly qualifies as a behavior problem, but it's different from many other common behavior problems. While many toddlers bite, the causes vary, so many traditional discipline techniques do not work. Since biting is often associated with the toddler stage and many toddlers bite, task force members considered referring to biting as "normal" or "typical." They felt that both of these words implied something that all children would do, something providers should be looking for as an indication that a child's development was proceeding as it should. Logically, then, a child who didn't bite would be seen as a child who was not on target developmentally. Since that obviously isn't true, the task force decided not to use "normal" or "typical" to describe biting.

Task force members then tried thinking of biting from the providers' point of view and found that many of them considered it an "expected" behavior. Using the word "expected," however, didn't seem to be a very good way to talk with parents about biting. Most parents do not expect toddlers to bite, and it seemed unlikely that parents would want their children in a program that expected biting to occur. Calling biting "expected" seemed to portray it as unavoidable, which might imply to parents that it would be taken too lightly. It might even conjure up images of caregivers eagerly awaiting the "expected" biting.

The task force finally settled on describing biting as a toddler behavior that is "unfortunately not unexpected." This conveys the understanding that while biting is not something providers or administrators want for the children in their programs and not something they look forward to, the staff in good programs are not surprised by biting among toddlers and are prepared to address it.

However you refer to biting in your program, this experience taught us that it is necessary to talk about biting among staff members until you find words that make sense to everyone. In the process, you may uncover differences in your assumptions about biting that can make it difficult to reach consensus on a plan to address it.

Assumptions about Biting

Most people (certainly most parents) see biting as a behavior problem that must be punished. Some adults believe that biting is a "crime" that calls for "justice." According to this way of thinking, if there is no punishment, then the biter has "gotten away with it," and this cannot be allowed. Parents are often infuriated when they see their own child bruised by a bite mark and no evidence of anyone "serving time" for the "crime." They may express shock and disbelief when they ask what happened to the child who bit and learn that the child was told, "We don't bite," and then redirected to another area of the room. Many parents, and a number of providers, may want the child who bit to have to pay a price for biting. Punishment makes them feel that in at least some small way, justice has been served. This places tremendous pressure on administrators and programs to punish biting to the satisfaction of adults, both providers and parents. Programs focused on the needs of children, however, do not use techniques simply to satisfy the adults involved when those techniques are, in fact, inappropriate or ineffective with children. And there's a lot of research showing that punishment is not an effective response to *any* kind of behavior problem.

While the task force took the position that biting is never justified, they also recognized that most of the many reasons toddlers bite do not fall into traditional "crime and punishment" or even "problem behavior and consequences" models of addressing challenging behaviors. While everyone's goal is to help toddlers stop biting and learn other behavior, punishing the child who is biting does not help anyone—the child, the provider, or the parent—reach that goal. It's that simple. What *is* effective at helping toddlers stop biting? To answer that question, it's necessary to understand why toddlers bite and then find strategies and techniques that match the child's reason or reasons for biting. Only then will the biting stop.

The real challenge for programs is to address biting effectively with children and explain it effectively to adults. In this book you will find information, strategies, techniques, and suggestions to do just that.

Program Perspectives on Biting

Whatever a program ultimately does about biting will be the result of the program staff's perspective on biting. Our perspectives reflect our beliefs, our attitudes, and our values. Our perspectives shape our goals, and our actions always flow from our goals.

Programs and providers who view biting only as a behavior problem will probably respond by disciplining the child. Their actions are likely to be punishments, which, as mentioned earlier, have been shown to be ineffective in stopping biting. Similarly, programs and providers who believe that toddlers bear all the responsibility for biting will respond by trying to fix the child. They will focus on getting the child to change and will not consider that their environment or practices may be a factor in the biting. On the other hand, programs and providers who believe that biting is "inevitable" will respond by "waiting out" the biting or hoping it won't get too bad. They may not take any action because they don't think they can do anything about it, since they believe biting is inevitable. Meanwhile, toddlers are injured, frightened, and confused, and parents are upset because biting continues and no one seems to know how to help or what to do.

If programs and providers want to be successful in dealing with biting, they must approach it in ways that are appropriate for children, families, and staff members. This is most likely to happen when they operate from a multidimensional perspective like this one:

- We understand and accept that when toddlers are in groups, biting is unfortunately not unexpected.
- We know and accept that toddlers bite for many reasons.
- We believe that biting is never the right thing to do.
- We want to help children who are bitten feel better by giving them care, support, and advice.
- We want children who bite to learn different, more appropriate behaviors.
- We understand that our caregiving environment and practices can influence biting, and we take responsibility for ensuring they are appropriate for toddlers.

- We understand that biting is very difficult for parents, and we communicate with them thoughtfully and frankly.

This perspective leads to two very worthwhile goals: to support toddlers whether they bite or are bitten and to support parents when biting occurs. With these goals in mind, you'll be less likely to look for the one perfect technique to implement, the one-size-fits-all plan for whenever biting occurs. Instead, as a professional you will approach each instance of biting from a problem-solving perspective. You will take into account developmental factors, treat each toddler as a unique individual, and look critically at the role of your caregiving environment in supporting or discouraging biting. That way, you'll always have alternatives, unlike the people locked into their one "perfect" technique, who inevitably find themselves not knowing what to do when it doesn't work. You will be like a master craftsperson who designs a plan for each specific situation and carefully carries out that plan.

This book is based on that perspective, and we recommend it to you as you work to address the biting dilemmas in your program appropriately and effectively.

How to Use This Book

The book is organized into three main sections. Chapters 1, 2, and 3 address the problem itself: why toddlers bite, how to respond when they do, how to help both the child who is biting and the child who is being bitten, and how to develop a plan to deal with repeated biting. This part of the book will help you handle your foremost concern—the children.

Perhaps just as important in controlling biting is how you talk with parents and other caregivers. The second section, chapters 4 and 5, contains information on how parents see biting, how to talk with them about it, and how to respond to their suggestions and demands. It also addresses how biting affects adults other than parents—other staff members, even members of the larger community.

The final section, chapter 6, focuses on creating policies about biting. We know that programs and providers need to have policies in place *before* biting becomes a problem. To do this, policymakers need the information, experiences, and suggestions presented in the first two sections of the book to create policies that will work well for their program as well as for children, staff, and parents.

Why Do Toddlers Bite?

Why *do* toddlers bite? It may be tempting to say, "I don't care *why* they bite; I just want them to stop." This reaction is certainly understandable, but it won't make the biting stop. Understanding why a toddler is biting is the first step to helping her stop. Often, nonetheless, adults insist, "She bit for no reason!" This reflects a view of toddler biting that is based on (and limited to) what makes sense and is apparent to the adult. Adults can understand that a toddler might bite when another child takes a toy away or hits. In the absence of such obvious reasons, however, many adults are baffled. They don't have the information or the understanding they need to work effectively with the toddler. It is important for us to acknowledge that there is always a reason for the biting. It is our role and responsibility to identify the reason or reasons so we can work effectively with each child. The approach you take to help a child stop biting depends on knowing why she is biting in the first place.

Three Categories of Causes for Biting

Toddlers bite for many reasons, and these fall into three broad categories:

1. Developmental issues, such as
   - Teething pain or discomfort
   - Developing oral-motor skills
   - Sensory exploration of the surroundings
   - Learning about cause and effect
   - Learning through imitating others
   - Developing a sense of space
   - Developing autonomy
   - Developing expressive communication skills

- Needing more attention
- Learning to hold on and let go
- Developing sensory integration
2. Expression of feelings, which may include
   - Frustration
   - Anger
   - Tension
   - Anxiety
   - Excitement
   - A reaction to abuse or other physical aggression
3. An environment or program that is not working for the child, for example
   - An environment that is too stimulating or not stimulating enough
   - A space that is too crowded and does not allow children privacy
   - Inappropriate expectations (such as expecting toddlers to share toys or equipment)
   - A rigid schedule that does not meet toddlers' needs for food and sleep

It takes thoughtful observation to find out why a particular toddler is biting. Any one or a combination of the above reasons may be involved. These reasons are not a checklist that an adult can look at briefly to decide why a child is biting, but rather a guide to many possibilities. It's possible to know what's going on with a particular child only by carefully watching him over time. On the following pages we take a look at these broad categories to give you an idea of why a child might bite.

Developmental Reasons for Biting

It is very important to understand that many of the reasons for biting are related to development. It helps to explain why we see so much biting in groups of toddlers but not in groups of preschoolers. It also puts biting into perspective: it points away from blaming toddlers for biting and toward understanding that while they are developing important knowledge and skills, biting is "not unexpected."

You are likely to notice that many of the developmental reasons for biting are interrelated. For example, toddlers are working on developing a sense of themselves as separate individuals with some power and control. At the same time, they often don't have the language skills to express themselves. Language skills are related to the development of oral-motor skills, which are necessary for speech. So a child may become frustrated when she feels powerless, such as when another child has a toy she wants. When she can't express herself verbally, she becomes even more frustrated. It may be the frustration that leads a child to bite, but the frustration is rooted in developmental considerations.

Teething. Some toddlers bite because of the pain and discomfort of teething. This is especially true of young toddlers, who may not make the distinction between a teething ring that feels good on sore gums and an arm that feels just as good. It is not usually difficult to recognize when a toddler is biting because of teething; she is most likely gnawing on just about everything.

Oral-Motor Skills. Another reason toddlers gnaw and may bite is because they are developing the oral-motor skills they need to eat without choking. At the toddler stage, this includes a great deal of chewing. They are exploring and experimenting with movement involving their mouths just as they do with other parts of their body. When toddler biting is related to developing oral-motor skills, we often see a great deal of oral-motor activity. Toddlers seek opportunities for oral stimulation: they put toys in their mouths and gum or chew them, they seek out activities that involve oral-motor skills such as blowing bubbles, and they often prefer foods they can chew over softer foods.

Sensory Exploration. Toddlers may bite because they are exploring: they learn about objects and people using all their senses. This means they like to discover how things feel and taste in their mouths. It isn't too surprising when the exploration goes from mouthing to tasting to chomping. Observing this progression helps you know when a toddler is using biting as a way of exploring.

Cause and Effect. Toddlers may bite because they are learning about cause and effect: "What happens when . . . ?" This natural developmental curiosity may become, "What happens when I sink my teeth into Laura's arm?" A toddler who bites while he is learning about cause and effect usually does not appear to be upset before he bites. He also may look quite surprised when the child he is biting reacts loudly to being bitten.

Imitation. Toddlers may bite because they are imitating others. Toddlers use imitation as a way to learn. They learn many behaviors from other children, and biting can be one of them. Caregivers often report that after a period of time of no biting, one child bites, and the next thing they know, they have an epidemic. When this happens, children may well be biting in imitation of others. Toddlers might also imitate biting behaviors they learn from adoring, but unwitting, parents and grandparents. Who hasn't heard parents and grandparents look at infants and toddlers and proclaim, "You are just so wonderful I could eat you up"? The adult then follows this proclamation by pretending to nibble or gobble the wonderfully plump cheeks, tummy, or thighs of a delighted child. It is hardly surprising that toddlers try out the same behaviors. Unfortunately they missed the part when the adults covered their teeth with their lips before chomping! When biting is related to this kind of imitation, we often see toddlers bite and then look to us with a big smile and an expression that seems to convey, "You are wonderful too. I could just eat you up!" Many caregivers find this is the situation when toddlers bite them.

Spatial Relationships. Toddlers may bite because they are developing an understanding of space and how it works. Toddlers are not able to judge a space or a distance by sight alone. To gain an understanding of space and spatial relationships, they must experiment physically, both with their own bodies and with materials—for example, by putting objects into containers and by trying to fit themselves into different spaces. With these kinds of experiments, they often end up on top of each other, and one child may become upset when another toddler gets too close. So biting can happen when children are too close together or when one child tries to get into the space already occupied by another. When biting is related to problems of physical closeness, a toddler may send a warning message by protesting when someone gets too close to him.

Autonomy. Toddlers may bite because of their developing understanding of autonomy. They are experimenting with asserting themselves as independent beings, and they are making choices and trying to control situations and other people. Some toddlers bite to demonstrate this control and to have power over others. It is quite easy to recognize when toddlers are trying to sort out autonomy—just listen for lots of "No!" "Mines!" and "Me do it!"

Language Limitations. Toddlers may bite because they don't have the language skills to express themselves. Because they are working on developing a sense of autonomy, they may have very definite ideas of what they want but not have the language to express those ideas. They don't have the words to convey their emotions, their needs, or their desires. It is very difficult for them to experience any control when other people do not understand what they want. The resulting frustration may cause them to express themselves by biting.

Attention. Toddlers may bite because they want and need more attention. Toddlers who need more attention than they are getting may notice that biting usually results in lots of attention. They would rather get the attention associated with biting—even if it is not pleasant—than get little or no attention.

It is very important to recognize that the need for attention belongs to the individual. We may feel that a child is getting plenty of attention and doesn't need any more. Toddlers, however, do not base their desire for attention on what we think should be enough! If we purposefully withhold attention, toddlers may bite even more.

Holding On and Letting Go. Sometimes biting is related to maturation of the central nervous system, which allows toddlers to control the muscles that hold on and let go. At first the muscles that hold on are stronger than the muscles that let go. We see this in potty training, where toddlers learn to "hold it" until they get to the potty and then let go of the urine and feces. Toddlers are also working on emotional holding on and letting go. We see evidence of this in separation anxiety, when toddlers struggle with letting go of their parents. Biting can be evidence of learning to hold on and let go at another level. We see this when a toddler who might have been mouthing another child's arm suddenly finds that his teeth are holding onto the arm even though he didn't mean to bite. This is often frightening to both children.

Sensory Integration. Sensory integration is the ability to use our senses to take in, sort out, and connect information from the world around us in an organized way. When toddlers cannot organize the information they take in through their senses, it is difficult for them to respond with appropriate behavior. For example, toddlers who have problems with sensory integration may bite because they find ordinary movements frightening. They may end up biting someone when that was not what they meant to do. Children who need lots of sensory input may even bite themselves.

Expressive Reasons for Biting

Frustration. Toddlers may bite because they are frustrated. This frustration is sometimes related to their lack of language skills. Toddlers are working on language development, but when they know exactly what they want and don't yet have the words to make themselves understood, their frustration can mount and result in a chomp. Toddlers are just barely beginning to develop inner control, and when frustration becomes too great, they may bite.

Anger. Toddlers may bite to express their anger. When toddlers can't get people or objects to do what they want, they can easily become angry. Biting in this situation has been called an "oral tantrum." When toddlers bite out of frustration or anger, you can often see their frustration or anger building before the actual bite occurs.

Tension. Toddlers may bite to release tension. When people are under pressure, their bodies tend to become very tense. Toddlers may bite to relieve the tension in their mouths and jaws.

Anxiety. Toddlers may bite because they are feeling anxious. When toddlers are feeling insecure, scared, or confused about something at home or in the child care program, they may relieve the anxiety by biting. Many adults also use oral solutions to relieve anxiety—for example, smoking, eating, or drinking.

Excitement. Toddlers may bite because they are excited. Some toddlers get so excited they can't contain themselves. In the excitement of the moment, they just might joyously sink their teeth into a body part that is close to them. When one little boy seemed to be targeting a particular girl for biting, the staff at the center finally asked him, "Why do you bite Mary?" He jumped up and down, clapped his hands and blurted out, "I just lub her!"

Self-protection. Toddlers may bite as a reaction to a physical act that is happening to them. If a toddler is being abused, he may react by being physically aggressive, and this may include biting. If a child in group care is bitten many times, she may also begin to bite.

Environmental Reasons for Biting

Overstimulation. Toddlers may bite because they are overwhelmed by too much stimulation. There may be too many toys and materials; the environment may be too noisy; lights may be too bright; the schedule may be too rushed; there may not be enough time to relax. Toddlers become stressed, and stressed toddlers may bite.

Boredom. Toddlers may also bite because the program is not stimulating enough! They may become bored if they don't have enough toys, materials, or interaction with adults. Boredom is another kind of stress that leads to conflicts.

Overcrowding. Toddlers may bite because the space is too crowded and lacks enough private places to retreat to. Toddlers often find all kinds of small spaces to crawl into, but sometimes the room is arranged in such a way that all the children end up on top of each other. When children aren't able to find ways to remove themselves from the group, their frustration may result in biting.

Developmentally Inappropriate Expectations. Toddlers may bite when the program has inappropriate expectations—for example, if they are expected to share toys and there are no duplicates of popular or newly introduced toys. Toddlers usually have not reached a developmental level at which they can share toys or use them to play with other children.

Scheduling Issues. Toddlers may bite if the program schedule doesn't meet their needs. When toddlers must wait too long, when they become overtired or hungry, they are likely to bite. Because toddlers, like all people, have varying needs for food and sleep and different capacities for waiting, a flexible program that allows toddlers to eat and sleep on their own schedule is more likely to meet most of their needs most of the time than one that is rigid.

Preventing Biting

The lists in these three categories make it clear why, despite their best efforts, teachers cannot guarantee there won't be any biting in toddler programs. Toddlers bite for so many reasons that it is not possible to predict or prevent every bite. At the same time, children are more likely to bite when they are under stress or when their needs are not being met in the program. For this reason, teachers' expectations of children, interactions with children, and the program's physical environment and daily schedule can affect how likely children are to bite. This is especially true when one or two incidents of biting expand into a biting epidemic. When environments, schedules, expectations, and interactions don't match toddler development, we can expect to struggle with biting. Not only is biting more likely to occur, but it is also more difficult to respond to effectively. The rest of this chapter suggests things you can do to help prevent biting and make it easier to respond to a child who is biting.

Provide a Supportive Environment

- Have duplicates of new toys and popular toys to reduce frustration.
- Keep popular toys available, but avoid overstimulation by making sure all the toys aren't available to the children at once. Rotate toys: store some away for a while, then bring them back out and put others away.
- Provide enough of the kind of stimulation that is important to toddlers. This includes many positive, individual interactions with them.

- Provide small, private spaces where children can go to be alone. You still need to be able to see them, but they need to feel that they are alone. Toddlers are working on understanding spatial relationships; that's why they like to try fitting themselves into small spaces.
- Provide several soft areas in the room. Use pillows, rugs, and comfortable upholstered furniture to provide coziness.
- Have safe materials visible and available at the children's level so they can use them without adult assistance.
- Create a variety of activity centers to discourage toddlers from bunching up in one area. Staff should spread themselves throughout the space; children often want to be where the adults are.
- Keep some of the activity areas and materials that toddlers find most interesting available throughout the day.
- Provide a menu that includes foods toddlers can gum, munch, and chew. Examples include banana chunks, soft tortilla strips, bagel pieces, and soft raw vegetables such as zucchini, lettuce, and spinach leaves.

Provide a Consistent yet Flexible Schedule

- Keep the daily schedule consistent, so it is predictable for children. Being able to predict what comes next is empowering.
- Simplify the daily routine and allow for flexibility to meet children's individual needs. Children need to eat when they are hungry and sleep when they are tired, regardless of whether it's snack- or naptime.
- Talk with the children about unavoidable changes in the schedule and be understanding of their reactions.
- Provide several opportunities each day for children to go outside.
- Keep waiting time to a minimum. Most teachers believe that waiting times in their program are very short, and they are surprised when they learn how long toddlers actually wait between activities. Try asking an objective person to observe your program and keep track of actual waiting time in minutes. To put the waiting time into perspective, take the number of minutes toddlers must wait, multiply by ten, and reflect on how you would react to that waiting time in that situation. For example, if the actual waiting time between the end of an activity and lunch is seven minutes, consider how you would respond to a seventy-minute wait in a similar situation. And remember: you would be expected to be still, be quiet, and be good during those seventy minutes.

- Take the time to go through the daily routine calmly, and don't rush children through activities or routines. This includes naptime. It is very unfair to toddlers to wake them up while they are sound asleep simply because afternoon snack is at one thirty.

Provide a Variety of Sensory Activities and Materials

- Provide a wide variety of soothing materials and activities, such as scarves and dress-up clothes that are soft and silky and cleaned often. Have sensory activities like painting and working with playdough available every day. The sand and water table should be available to toddlers at least several times a week. If your program doesn't have a sand and water table, you can use small individual basins.
- Provide activities and materials for oral stimulation and for practicing oral-motor skills. Examples include bubbles and musical instruments that make sounds when blown into.
- Provide many cause-and-effect toys that toddlers can act on to make them "do something." Musical instruments, busy boxes, pounding boards, and jack-in-the-boxes are all examples of cause-and-effect toys.
- Provide opportunities for toddlers to put collections of small, choking-safe objects (for example, clothespins, jar lids, juice can lids) in containers, carry them around, and then dump them out. This is a favorite toddler activity and, if indulged, soon progresses to the point at which they can begin to learn about picking up.
- Instead of planning teacher-directed activities, offer interesting materials and experiences. Observe the children's reactions to the materials and then plan how to further their interest. Offer the same thing over and over, so that children have many opportunities to experiment.
- Offer adult-initiated activities that are spontaneous, short, and optional such as songs, stories, and fingerplays.
- Do not expect toddlers to have formal circle time or to sit throughout whole-group activities.

Interact with Children Gently and Empathetically

- Show children what empathy looks like and sounds like; model it in your interactions with them.
- Respond positively to children.
- Help children identify and name their feelings. Say things such as, "Ramon, you look sad to me. Are you feeling sad right now?" or

"Robin, you look frustrated to me. You really wanted to play with that truck, and Sonja has it."

- Show and tell children how to use language to express feelings and state their needs and wants. Say things such as, "Robin, you can tell Sonja, 'My turn next.' That way she knows you're waiting for the truck."
- Encourage children to comfort themselves by using transitional items like stuffed animals or blankets brought from home or by sucking their thumb or pacifier (if that is what they already do to comfort themselves).
- Comfort children with soothing voice tone and physical actions such as hugs, gentle hands on their shoulders, and back rubs.
- Help children fix mistakes. For example, if a child looks genuinely upset that she hurt another, you can say, "Sammy, you look upset that Lonetta is crying. I wonder if she'd like a hug?" Other possible ways to fix a mistake include helping to rebuild a knocked-down tower, kissing a "boo-boo," fetching ice for a bite, and saying you're sorry (do not impose apologies; they should come from a child's own feelings and not be an adult-imposed formula).
- Give attention in a generous and genuine manner.

Despite the best efforts of the best caregivers to prevent it, biting still (unfortunately) happens. When it does occur, toddler caregivers must be prepared to respond appropriately and effectively. The next chapter shows you how.

What to Do When Toddlers Bite

What most caregivers want to know is, "What do I *do* when a toddler bites?" Unfortunately, there is no simple answer. As the introduction noted, because toddlers bite for a variety of reasons and in a variety of circumstances, there is no one-size-fits-all response to biting. The response that helps a child stop biting and keeps other children safe is different depending on each child's needs, temperament, and reason for biting.

To determine the best response in a given situation, teachers must observe the child closely to find out why he is biting. While gathering this information, pay attention to the environmental factors that might be encouraging the biting and try to prevent as many further bites as possible. The next chapter will tell you what to do when you have a pattern of ongoing biting in your program or when the same child bites repeatedly. This chapter focuses on what to do in the moment after a child has been bitten. The immediate response should always be the same, whether it's the first time the child has bitten or his seventh bite that day.

Whenever you're dealing with biting, you need to act quickly and directly. You want your words, attitudes, and actions to convey a strong message:

- Biting is not the right thing to do.
- You will help the child who was bitten feel better.
- You will help the child who bit learn different, more appropriate behavior.

When you are responding to individual biting incidents, you probably won't see the actual bite—only the aftermath. Nevertheless, by looking at the two children you can usually get some idea of the circumstances. For example, children who bite because they are exploring, mouthing, or experimenting with cause and effect may look rather surprised at the outraged cries of their victims. When children bite out of frustration or anger, you may see evidence of their feelings in their voices, facial expressions, or body language.

If you see one child triumphantly holding a toy while another child with bite marks on her arm is crying and pointing to the toy, you have a pretty good idea of what happened.

At this point, you have to decide where to go and what to say. On some occasions, you will want to separate the children; at other times you will want the children to be near each other while you deal with the biting. Separate the children when emotions are still high and you worry that more biting will take place if the children remain near each other. Pay attention to the feelings of the child who was bitten:

- If she is scared or worried, separate her from the child who bit her, even if it's just positioning yourself between the two children.
- If she is furious and ready to retaliate, separate the children to prevent escalation.
- If she is indignant, you might bring both children together so the victim can express her outrage directly.

You can also use the reaction of the child who bit to help decide whether to separate the children. If he is calm, curious, or content after biting, it may be a good idea to have him nearby to see the negative effects of his biting.

If you decide to separate the children, either you must have two caregivers who can each attend to one child or one caregiver must attend to both children, one at a time. If you are attending to both children, you must decide whom to go to first. Unless the child who bit is in danger of hurting someone else, go to the child who was bitten first. Meanwhile, make sure the child who bit sees the aftermath of the biting as you tend to the child who was bitten. Without being punitive, tell the child who bit, "Stay right here for a minute." The more neutral you can be, the better—it's important that you not be angry or show other emotions. You're not giving him a time-out or punishing him in some way; you just want him to wait so you can finish interacting with him after you've cared for the child who was bitten.

Helping the Child Who Was Bitten

Check the bite and give the appropriate first aid (see pages 19–20 for first aid information). Comfort the child. Let the child know that you sincerely regret he was bitten, that it wasn't right. This can be a simple statement such as, "I'm sorry you got hurt" or "Maeko bit you, and that's not right." It is important for the child to hear this message. It affirms for the child that this is not something that should happen to him. The child may protest the bite in a manner that reflects his expressive language limitations. He may cry, jabber indignantly, or protest with words, phrases, or short sentences. Respond to these by acknowledging his feelings and letting him know he has every reason to protest. "You are right! That really hurt, and no one should bite you!" This helps children to know they have been heard and understood.

You can also tell the child what he can do to respond to the child who bit him. You shouldn't insist that he do it, but you can help the child understand that a response is possible and give him the language and the confidence to respond appropriately. This can be a short statement like, "You can tell Maeko no." You can also give the child advice about what to do if he is worried someone might be about to bite him. Tell the child, "If you're worried someone will hurt you, you can say, 'Stop!' or 'No!'" Teach the child to deliver this message in an emphatic tone of voice.

You can also teach him some effective body language. Show the child how to put his hand up, palm out, at arm's length in front of him while he says, "Stop!" Doing so helps prevent anyone coming toward him to bite from getting to the softer, fleshier parts that are easier to bite. Instead, the biter will encounter the palm of his hand, which is harder to bite. This is a powerful suggestion for the child who has been bitten. He doesn't have to wait until after he's been bitten to act. He doesn't have to guess whether the other child might bite him; he can act on his own feelings. Having an appropriate way to act on our feelings is empowering for all of us. This suggestion can also help prevent some bites. It may prevent a child from getting close enough to bite and give you time to intervene. When a child tries this behavior, go to him and let him know he is doing it correctly. "Good for you. You were worried she might hurt you, and you said, 'Stop.' That's exactly right." You can further reinforce this by telling the child who may have been about to bite, "He just said 'Stop!' and I have to say, it looks like he means it! Let's find something else for you to do."

Finally, take your cue from the child to decide what other steps may be needed to help him. He may want to stay close to you for a while, he may want to be near other children, or he may want to play alone in a quiet space.

✚ FIRST AID FOR BITES

The Task Force on Biting contacted Dr. Gary Johnson, associate professor of emergency medicine at University Hospital in Syracuse, New York, for information on treating bites in child care settings. He advises that if the skin is not broken, you don't have to worry about infection. However, the bite may still hurt quite a bit, and you may want to offer to put ice on it. Some programs keep ice in small packs or "boo-boo bunnies" (washcloths folded to look like a bunny with pouch for an ice cube) available for such use. Other programs use frozen sponges; wet paper towels in small, sealed plastic bags; frozen teething rings; or bags of frozen vegetables. The frozen vegetables seem to be very popular because they can be molded to shapes of various body parts!

If the skin is broken, you need to clean the wound. First, wash your own hands thoroughly. If the wound is bleeding, apply direct pressure to stop the bleeding. Then clean the wound with soap and water. Antibiotic creams and ointments can help prevent infections. (Note: Child care program regulations vary from state to state. Check your state's regulations and your program's policies on the use of over-the-counter ointments before using them.) After the wound is cleaned, exposure to open air is optimal. If the wound is bleeding or if the child is likely to get dirt in it, cover it with a bandage.

You need to be especially concerned with bites that break the skin on the top of the hand and on the fingers because bacteria may come into contact with tendons. Dr. Johnson recommends that when such bites occur, children should be seen by medical personnel.

The issue of biting can be further inflamed when adults call the human mouth "the filthiest of all mouths." This language is especially upsetting because we think of biting as an animal, not a human behavior. According to the Mayo Clinic's Web site, human bites "can be as dangerous or even more dangerous" than the bites of animals because of the "types of bacteria and viruses contained in the human mouth." This information seems to support the view that children who bite are indeed dangerous. However, there are many other ways that young children in group care spread bacteria and viruses to others, and we typically do not think of those ways as dangerous. We can best use this information to talk about the issue accurately and to focus on the importance of appropriate first aid for bites.

Helping the Child Who Bit

Once the child who was bitten is calm, you can turn to the child who bit. A toddler's attention span is usually quite short, so you want to do this within a minute or two. When you respond to the child who bit, be genuine, brief, and serious. Respond verbally and with an action, even when the action is something as simple as redirecting the child.

Your verbal response must clearly indicate that biting is not the right thing to do. This is not a time to laugh, snicker, or use any kind of humor. You don't want the child to get the impression that biting is cute or funny.

Use a genuine tone of voice that sounds serious without being threatening. This is especially important because toddlers may not understand all your words, but they will understand the tone of your voice, and that's what they will respond to. You can use serious words, but if your tone of voice is light and friendly, you are not sending a serious message. Many caregivers find that lowering both the pitch and the volume of their voice slightly while speaking firmly conveys a sense of seriousness. It's important to state briefly and clearly what happened and that the biting was not okay. This is especially helpful for toddlers because it enhances the language skills they are struggling to develop. Here are some examples of possible things to say to a child who has just bitten another child:

- "You bit him with your teeth. He doesn't like it. It's not okay to bite people." (By adding the words "with your teeth," this response clarifies the word "bit" for very young toddlers.)
- "You bit her, and it hurt her. That's why she's crying. I don't want you to bite anyone."
- "You were so mad when the truck wouldn't work! And you bit Trey. Biting hurts people. I'll help you when you're mad, but you may not bite people." "Emily had a toy you wanted, and you bit her to take it away. Biting hurts people, and you can't have toys when you bite people to get them."
- "You bit Ryan and hurt him. He was trying to get into your cubby with you. You can tell him, 'No, Ryan!' But there is no biting."
- "Oh, dear. You were trying to kiss Lee, but you hurt him with your teeth. Please be careful so you don't bite people."

Note that these responses are all very specific in describing what happened and why biting is not okay. They are different from "That's not nice," a response we often hear from caregivers. While indeed biting is not nice, such a response is too vague. It doesn't convey the understanding that biting is the wrong thing to do. Notice, too, that none of these responses refers to hurting "our friends." Rather, they refer to the child who was bitten by name. This makes it much more personal and specific. The children in a child care program are not necessarily all friends, nor do they need to be. When we use phrases such as "We don't bite our friends," the underlying message is that while we don't bite people who are identified as our friends, other people are fair game!

Avoid using verbal responses that are outrageous, untrue, or frightening for toddlers. Telling a toddler that all her teeth will fall out if she bites, for example, is both unfair to the child (because it is untrue) and ineffective in stopping the biting.

Tie Your Verbal Response to an Action Response

The verbal response should almost always be followed by an action response. The action you choose to take must fit the circumstances of the incident, but it may also include advice and actions for the child to try. As we have seen, biting is not usually an intentional act. It often occurs when toddlers have trouble with what they are trying to accomplish. While we want to send the message that biting is not the right thing to do, we also need to direct toddlers to what we *do* want them to do.

If you take a moment to try to understand what the toddler was thinking, you can gain insight that will help you give her advice. Here's an example. Suppose Anna is playing with a shape sorter. She tries and tries to get the square shape into the round hole. She pounds harder and harder. Malik toddles over to her and reaches for the shape sorter, and Anna bites him on the arm. Suppose you deal effectively with both Malik and Anna as described earlier in this chapter. You can take an additional action step that will be very helpful to Anna. If you consider this situation, you realize that Anna thought she would be able to get the square shape into the round hole. She tried it, but it didn't work. So she tried a different strategy—she pounded harder. That didn't work either. Her frustration was building, and she eventually bit. If you were to give Anna some advice about the shape sorter, you could help her develop skills to prevent frustration. "Anna, here's what I know about the shape sorter. When one piece doesn't fit, maybe another piece will." You can then spend a few minutes with Anna and the shape sorter, helping her use your advice to experiment and problem solve. In this instance, you have crafted a response that not only addresses the behavior but also helps the child learn a new strategy to solve a problem and avoid frustration.

If the biting was a matter of mouthing or exploration, a caregiver can demonstrate how to touch without hurting. Use gentle or other appropriate touches on the child who just bit and, in some cases, on the child who was bitten. Don't insist that the child who bit try out the gentle touches on the child who was just bitten. The timing may not be right. Be sure to include lots of language with your demonstrations. Here are some examples:

- "I'm going to use my fingers to touch your arm. Your arm feels smooth and warm. I don't use my teeth on your arm."
- "You can use your hand to touch Juan's cheek if he wants you to."
- "I'll touch your hand like this so you will know how to touch Libby's hand."

When a child's biting is related to anger, a caregiver can help him learn the words, tone of voice, and body language to express anger in a powerful but safe manner. Depending on the child's language ability, teach him to say phrases such as, "Oh no!" or "I'm so mad!" or "The truck wouldn't work right!" in an emphatic tone of voice. Show him how to add emphatic body language by putting his hands on his hips or crossing his arms over his chest with great gusto. When you see and hear him use such expressions, tone, and body language to express anger, let him know, "That's exactly the way to do it. I could tell that you were really mad. Good for you."

Sometimes a toddler caregiver has the child who bit help care for the child who was just bitten. This typically involves getting a wet cloth or holding a frozen sponge on the bite for the other child. While this can be very effective for both children, you need to take your cue from the children, particularly the child who was bitten. It should be up to the child who was bitten to accept or refuse the help; this gives her at least a small measure of control, which is important after not being able to control being bitten. The child who bit may also balk or refuse to help take care of the bite he just inflicted. Insisting that a child in these circumstances must help take care of the other child is not likely to be very effective. In addition, it isn't very reassuring or comforting to the child who was just bitten to find that she is going to be taken care of by someone who is resistant or belligerent.

APOLOGIES

Should we ever require the child who bit to apologize? Many caregivers try to have older toddlers say "I'm sorry" to the child they bit. The thought behind this practice is to teach children to be accountable for their behavior by apologizing. While this may be a good motive, the practice is not a good fit for toddlers or for biting. When older toddlers are reminded or forced to say "I'm sorry" in situations in which their behavior was inappropriate, they can readily learn to utter the words. They can even learn the correct contrite tone of voice. It does not guarantee, however, that they feel remorse for hurting someone else or that they are consciously taking responsibility for their behavior. Some older toddlers will dutifully say, "I'm sorry," and turn right around and bite again. When this happens, caregivers and parents might interpret it as meaning that the child knows biting is wrong and bites anyway. They may view the child as biting intentionally, with premeditated malice. This interpretation is likely to result in very ineffective responses from adults that focus on punishing the child rather than teaching him other ways of expressing himself or dealing with his emotions.

When a child utters the required words of apology, adults consider the matter settled and do not spend any time working on helping the child learn different behavior or considering changes that should be made to the environment to help reduce biting. Over time children learn that it's all right to hurt other people as long as they say "I'm sorry" afterward. Adults don't intend for this to be the lesson children learn, but often it is. Ironically, it's also the very opposite of genuinely taking responsibility for their own behavior.

Another good action to take after responding verbally to a child who bit is redirection—directing a toddler's attention to a different toy, activity, person, or area of the room. Redirection is most likely to work well when it is specific. Telling a toddler "You need to find something else to do" doesn't work nearly as well as "This doll needs a ride in the buggy" or "I see Rhonda getting the fingerpaints out." Fortunately, most toddlers are easily redirected.

In some cases, toddlers may insist on doing what you're pretty sure is going to lead to another bite or continuing to do what led to the bite in the first place. When you try to redirect them, they may be resistant. You may want to combine several strategies. For example, you can

- acknowledge their feelings (and the depth of their feelings); say something such as, "You really want to hug Jessie, but she doesn't want you to hug her right now," or "You really want to be in that cubby, but Tyrone is in there right now."
- redirect them; say something such as, "I wonder if Sydney would like a hug instead?" or "Tyrone's in the cubby, but I see an empty place under the loft," or "Carmen has the blue ball, but I see a big red ball on the floor."
- give them choices; say something such as, "You could see if Sydney wants a hug, or give me a big hug," or "You could go in that empty space under the loft or try fingerpainting with Rhonda," or "You could play with the big red ball, or play at the water table with Niki."

Here is an example of how it might work when you put all three redirection strategies together: "You wish you could stay here and get into the cubby with Tyrone. But only one person can be in the cubby at a time. You can go in a different cubby, or you can play with the trucks."

These responses help children who have just bitten understand that biting is not the right thing to do and that you will help them learn different, more appropriate behavior.

A child should never profit by biting. If a child bites to get a toy away from another child, he should not be allowed to keep the toy. Even if the other child quickly forgets about the toy, taking the toy away helps send the message that biting is not the right thing to do. This also helps toddlers learn about cause and effect.

What Not to Do

Because biting is such a problem in toddler programs, adults are always looking for and are willing to try almost any suggestion to deal with it.

They often try techniques that they have heard about (but not really thought about) only to discover that they're not very effective. This is frustrating for everyone and often leads to claims such as, "We've tried everything, and nothing works!" Here are some of those failed techniques along with explanations about why they are ineffective.

Time-Out

One technique that is often suggested or tried with young children in programs is time-out. Not being allowed to participate in an activity may make sense to adults as a punishment, and it might even serve to eliminate an older child's misbehavior. A time-out makes sense to us as adults because we can connect the punishment to the behavior. Toddlers, however, do not experience a time-out in the same way because they don't make that connection. As the developmental psychologist Jean Piaget reminds us, the way young children think and reason is different from the way older children and adults think and reason.

Trying to put a toddler in a time-out after biting may be as frustrating for the adult as it is for the child. The toddler can't figure out why the adult is so insistent that she sit, and the adult can't figure out why the toddler won't stay in time-out. The end result is a battle between the adult and the toddler.

Some adults believe time-out offers an opportunity for children to think about what they did. Can any of us really imagine toddlers who have bitten thinking to themselves, "Oh, dear. I was frustrated because I don't have the language to express my feelings. I took it out on another child by biting. I hurt this other child, and now I feel very sorry for doing it. I should not do this and will never do it again!"?

Caregivers may still protest that a toddler "knows what she's doing is wrong because whenever she bites she goes over and sits in the time-out chair." This was observed in one program in which a child of twenty months had been biting. The caregivers had been using time-outs with this child and were frustrated because while time-outs "seemed to be working," the little girl was still biting. During the observation, the little girl was tussling over a toy with another toddler, a boy of about the same age and size. After a brief struggle, the little girl bit the boy, who promptly let go of the toy. The little girl then took herself to the time-out chair, where she sat playing with the very toy she had bitten to get. After a few moments she got up and returned to the group, still playing with the toy. The caregiver was convinced that the girl realized that biting was bad because she went to the time-out chair voluntarily. The caregiver was frustrated because even though the child had "served time" for her "crime," she was still biting.

To the outside observer, it was obvious that the girl had learned that biting was followed by a short sit-down period. Putting herself in a time-out had nothing to do with knowing or caring that she had hurt another child. Rather, time-outs had become part of the biting routine. And we know that routines are very important and powerful to toddlers.

Saying, "How Would You Like It . . . ?"

Sometimes when toddlers bite, adults say to them, "How would you like it if he bit you?" Variations of this technique include "Would you want someone to bite you?" and "Do you like it when people bite you?"

If they respond to these questions at all, most toddlers will say, "No." And truly, they *wouldn't* want someone to bite them, and they *don't* like it when people bite them.

Having gotten toddlers to agree that they wouldn't want to be bitten, adults then take the next logical step, which is to say, "Well, then, if you would not want to be bitten, probably the child you just bit didn't want to be bitten either." This makes sense to adults because it is the next logical step. And this is exactly why it doesn't work with toddlers. They don't make that logical step because they don't think logically. Logic is one of the characteristics of the thinking of older children and adults, not of young children.

So if you get a toddler to agree that he would not want to be bitten, you really can't expect him to make the connection to not biting another child. And because he doesn't make that connection, your saying, "Would you like it if . . . ?" is not very effective in stopping him from biting.

Lecturing or Going on a Tirade

Sometimes adults respond to biting by telling the child at length what she did wrong and why (a lecture) or by telling her over and over again, with a lot of emotion, not to do something (a tirade). These are both ineffective in stopping biting behavior. Adults may lecture or go off on tirades because it makes them feel as if they are doing something about the biting. It also can release the tension they may feel about the biting incident. (Ironically, toddlers may also be trying to relieve tension by biting. A tirade might be thought of as an adult version of biting!)

Lectures are ineffective because they are usually too long and not given in toddler-friendly language. Children lose track of what an adult is talking about very quickly, especially in an emotional situation. They need to hear briefly and clearly what happened, what was wrong, and what to do next.

Tirades are ineffective because the adult's voice and body language frighten or surprise children, and the message usually gets lost. Remember: adding to children's stress increases the chance they will bite someone. In some tirades, the word "bite" or "biting" is used so often and with such emphasis that it might actually sound like a cheer urging on children to bite. Here's an example:

"You just bit her. There is no biting here. Biting is very bad. Biting hurts other people. We don't bite. Do you want someone to bite you? Don't bite! Don't bite! Don't bite! Do you hear me? Do not bite!"

Delivered in a loud, passionate voice, a tirade can be intense enough to make anyone—especially a toddler—feel like chomping something. Adults need to be aware that just because they feel better after they have delivered a lecture or tirade doesn't mean that they have affected the biting at all.

Handling Ongoing Biting

Isolated biting incidents are difficult enough. Many caregivers feel overwhelmed when the biting becomes repeated, involves more than one child, or seems to go on and on. When you are faced with patterns of biting, you need to develop a plan that involves observation and reflection and uses specific strategies and techniques. These strategies and techniques should be identified and chosen because they are a good match for the patterns and situations you are facing. This chapter will help you develop a plan to cope with ongoing biting and carry it out step by step. It addresses situations in which more than one child may be biting as well as those in which the same child bites repeatedly.

In order to make a plan, you need to gather some information by

1. observing the children who are biting;
2. consulting with the parents of the children who are biting;
3. observing and reflecting on your program.

These three steps will help you gain insight into the biting. Without taking all of these steps, you will not be able to tailor your approach to the needs of the children who are biting, and that makes your plan less likely to succeed. Once you have gathered thorough information, you will be able to assess the problem and develop a comprehensive plan to address it.

Observe the Child

Note: The term "child" is used in this section, but the information applies whether several different children are biting or one child is biting repeatedly. The next section discusses additional considerations when you have one child who bites again and again.

Remember that long list of reasons why children bite in chapter 1? Observing the child as soon as you realize you have a biting problem in your program is the first step toward understanding why the child is biting. You need observations that will yield information about the biting incidents and information about the child's personality, development, interests, and style of interacting with the environment. Information about the biting incidents will help you discover patterns. Information about the child will show you how the child interacts with teachers, other children, and the environment. You will need to keep track of the following information for at least a week in order to have enough details about the child to make a good guess about what is going on.

Do the bites always happen at the same time of the day? (Maybe the child is hungry or tired then, or maybe it's an especially chaotic time in your schedule.) Do the bites happen at different times of the day, but always during a transition? (Maybe transitions are especially hard for the child.) Do the bites always happen in one part of the room? (Maybe that part of the room is drawing too many children, or there's a bottleneck there that's leading to frustration.) These, and many other possibilities, will be revealed as you keep track of what actually happens when the child bites. If more than one child is biting, you'll need to keep careful observations about each one.

Whenever a bite occurs, you need to fill out an incident report, which contains some of the information listed below (those items followed by an asterisk). Your observations of the child, however, must go beyond the immediate facts of the incident itself. Taken together, the incident reports and the observations of the child should include the following:

- When the bites have taken place*
- Where in the environment the bites have taken place*
- Whom the child has bitten*
- What was happening just before each bite*
- The child's reaction after biting*
- The child's social interaction skills
- The child's oral-motor skills
- The child's motor skills
- The child's general personality characteristics
- The child's chronological age

As you complete your observations, review them to see if you can find any patterns. Biting is rarely a random event; a child almost always bites for a reason. You may be able to find several patterns, perhaps one having to do with the time of the bites, another having to do with who is being bitten, or another having to do with where the child is in the room when she bites. Two examples of actual observations appear in appendix B. They were made during the course of typical mornings in child care settings. Each one contains observations, reflections, and insights into the child's biting and includes related recommendations to help reduce the biting. Be sure to notice any times or places in which biting does not occur. Often, for instance, caregivers discover that biting does not happen outside, perhaps because children have more space.

Special Considerations When One Child Bites Repeatedly

One of the most challenging situations in toddler care occurs when one child bites again and again. This is when it is especially important to focus on positive ways to help the child learn to stop biting. A very common and seemingly innocent practice often gets in the way: referring to the toddler who bites repeatedly as "the biter." Many caregivers insist that since the child *is* biting, it is fitting to refer to her as "the biter." There is a great deal of difference, however, between the way we think about "a child who is biting" and a child who is "a biter." Since our thoughts guide our actions, it is worth looking at this more closely.

It is unfair to the child to be labeled "a biter" or—even worse—"*the* biter." First, any label serves to define a child and shapes the way adults respond to and interact with her. The label "biter" portrays a child in a negative light and is likely to result in responses from adults that are less supportive and more negative—even if the adult is unaware of it. Second, the label is based on only one behavior—biting. We don't use such labels for other behaviors. A toddler who has frequent bowel movements is not called "the pooper." We don't refer to a child who often tips over her juice cup as "the spiller." Besides being unfair, labeling a child as "a biter" gets in the way of effective practices because it suggests that there may be little we, the adults, can do about the biting. It directs our attention on blaming the child and away from considering how to help the child learn not to bite. It also diverts our attention away from considering that some of our own practices and behaviors may be contributing to the biting. When a child is biting repeatedly, refer to her by name. Insist that others do the same and explain why. It seems like a small thing, but it really does matter.

When the same child bites repeatedly, adult frustrations often run very high. This is true of both parents and caregivers. Because the pressure is on, caregivers frequently respond by trying one technique after another with little thought given to whether any of them match the specific child and situation. Techniques are tried for a day or two and then replaced by others. When the biting continues, adults often throw up their hands, declaring, "We've tried everything, and nothing works." The implication is clear: since everything has been tried, nothing more can be done, and nothing more can be expected. This is when programs and staff feel justified in expelling a child.

To address this difficult situation, you need a plan that has been carefully and thoughtfully crafted to be appropriate for the child. Such a plan is based on careful observations of the child *in the child care environment* and on thoughtful reflection about how what you observe relates to biting. From there it is not difficult to craft a plan that is likely to be very effective.

Consult with the Parents

While you are gathering information about the child's biting, you will need to talk with her parents. From the incident reports, the parents will already know that their child has been biting, but you will want to tell them what you have noticed in your program and ask them what (if anything) they have noticed at home. Ask them if they have any insights into the biting or if they are aware of anything their child seems upset or worried about. Allow time and opportunity for parents to ask you questions too. You can tell them that you are keeping track of the biting to try to understand its pattern and that when you have enough information, you will be making a plan to address the biting. They will probably want to know how you handle the child after she bites, and they will probably need to be reassured that their child really is okay, not a monster! (See chapter 4 for more information about talking with parents.)

Reflect on the Program

Before you make a plan, you need to observe your program to find out how well it's working for the children, and particularly for the child who is biting. In what ways might your program be contributing to the biting? Examine your environment, materials, activities, schedule, and interactions with children. You can use the preventive measures mentioned on pages 13–16 as a checklist to complete this observation and reflection. You might ask your administrator to come in and observe as well.

Objective observation can be extremely difficult. In one program, teachers were frustrated when technique after technique failed to make a dent in the biting, which involved several children. Finally, an outside observer asked if there were any times at all during the day when there was no biting. At first the staff answered that there wasn't, but as they went through the daily schedule, they realized the biting did not occur when the children went outside. The teachers changed the schedule temporarily to go outdoors with the children three times during the day instead of just once. It was a big adjustment, but the biting stopped. The teachers then went on to look at the difference between the classroom and the outdoor environment. They realized that the classroom was very crowded and children were tripping over each other. They tried changing the room arrangement so children had more space to move about without getting in each other's way. With these changes, the biting stopped even when the children were inside.

Objective observation means being brutally honest with yourself, because the program has such a huge impact on the children. A biting problem can almost always be helped by a change in the program. If, for example, you rarely offer activities or materials such as sand and water play or painting because they are too messy, you are probably not providing adequate sensory experiences for the children. Sensory play is one of the most effective tools for preventing biting, and providing many opportunities for sensory play can have a huge impact on biting. If you don't like to offer sand and water play, find someone who can help increase your comfort level with this activity. As you discover ways to keep the mess minimal or easy to clean up, you may be less likely to limit the children's experiences. You will need every tool you can find to help the biting stop, and it's much easier to ask children and families to change their behavior when you yourself have been willing to make changes.

Develop a Plan

From your observations of the children and your conferences with parents, you can determine a possible reason or reasons the child may be biting. Your observation and reflection on your program will help you identify specific areas that may be contributing to the biting. Use the information you have gathered in these three steps to develop an action plan. Write down what specifically you are going to do to change your program, and what specific strategies you are going to use with the children. Write down the timeline and who is responsible for each part of the plan. For example, "We need more sensory experiences. The water table will be available every day. Janine will supervise it."

To address ongoing biting effectively, you will most likely need to implement program changes as well as specific techniques to help the child who is biting. What follows here are strategies and techniques tailored to some of the specific reasons children bite.

Strategies and Techniques Related to Development

Chapter 1 identified developmental issues that can provide context for biting. They include teething, oral-motor development, sensory exploration, learning cause and effect, imitation, spatial awareness, emerging autonomy, expressive language development, needing attention, and holding on and letting go. Here are some strategies and techniques for dealing with each.

TEETHING

- Check with parents to see what they are doing for their child's teething pain. If they are using something to soothe gums, ask them to bring a supply (with instructions) to use in the program. Be sure to consult your state's licensing regulations and your program's policy on the use of over-the-counter medications with children, especially medications that go in children's mouths.
- Make sure you have a variety of objects that children can chew on to relieve the pain and pressure of teething. These might include teething toys, frozen foods that are chewy and won't cause choking, and clean cloths that have been frozen.
- Actively encourage toddlers who are teething to bite on these items; you are telling children what you *do* want them to bite rather than simply telling them that you *don't* want them to bite other children after they've already done so.

ORAL-MOTOR DEVELOPMENT

- Provide many toys and materials that work by having children blow. These include bubble wands, rings, and pipes that children can use to blow bubbles; musical instruments that children blow into to produce sound; toys with tubes that children blow into to make small objects rise; party favors that unroll when children blow into them. Have children blow through straws to paint, to make small toy cars move, and so forth.
- Provide materials specifically for children to gnaw on. Some children may benefit from chewing on special toothbrushes such as Nuk brushes, which have soft bristles on one end and a hard nub on the other. These are different from teething rings because children can use their molars. Special care must be taken to ensure that children gnaw on only their own toothbrush and that gnawing toys are kept clean and sanitized.
- Provide foods with a variety of textures. Children need soft food such as cooked vegetables and bread to munch, hard foods such as toast and raw vegetable slices to crunch, and chewy foods such as fruits and diced meats to chew. Allow children enough time to munch, crunch, and chew their food.

SENSORY EXPLORATION

- Since toddlers often explore with their mouths, make sure you have a plentiful and varied supply of toys they *can* put in their mouths. Have a plan for cleaning such toys. One recommendation is to pick up any toy you have seen a child mouth and set it aside to be cleaned (that's why you need so many of them). The toys are then washed with soap and water, sprayed with a bleach-and-water solution (one part bleach to ten parts water), and left to air dry.

- Provide many opportunities and materials for sensory play. Offer supervised sand and water play. Have sensory art materials, such as fingerpaints and playdough, available for supervised exploration.
- Give children opportunities to explore a variety of textures, spaces, and places. Provide tunnels, small forts, and different kinds of surfaces for children to crawl on.

EXPERIMENTING WITH CAUSE AND EFFECT

- Provide toddlers with plenty of cause-and-effect toys. These include toys and activity books in which they can make something happen by pushing a button, turning a knob, lifting a flap, pulling a tab, and so on.
- Offer art materials so toddlers can make colors and designs appear by wielding a brush or marker.
- Help toddlers understand "What happens when . . ." and "What happens if . . ." by describing the cause-and-effect relationships you see a child engaging in. Use phrases such as:
  - "Look at that. When you moved the paintbrush across the paper, you made all that blue."
  - "Every time you pull the string, that little door opens, and you can see the clown."
- When a child bites, use cause-and-effect statements to describe the painful result of the biting such as, "When you bit Maura, it hurt her, and she cried." Make sure that the child does not profit from biting. Do not allow the child to keep a toy that was obtained by biting the child who originally had it. This way the child learns, "If you bite someone to get a toy, you can't keep the toy."
- Help toddlers recognize the cause and effect of positive behavior. "When you got more playdough, Isabel could use it, too, and she likes that." "When you helped pick up the toys, we got to go outside to play sooner."

IMITATING

- When you suspect a toddler might be biting because he is imitating another child, provide lots of examples of other, more acceptable behavior for the child to imitate. Model nurturing, sharing, respectful, polite, empathetic behavior. Show positive ways to handle anger and frustration. When you say, "I was so frustrated when I couldn't get the jar open," or when you respond to a child who is angry with "You are so angry with Tenzin because he took the truck you had," you are giving the child a new behavior to imitate.

- Stop any play biting that you may be doing with toddlers. Ask other adults to do the same. (See chapter 1 for more information on play biting.)

SPATIAL AWARENESS

- Recognize that toddlers like to experiment with space and provide them with many small areas that are just the right size for one. Allow toddlers to take toys off low shelves so they can sit on those shelves themselves.
- Create simple and safe obstacle courses so toddlers can experiment with going through cardboard box tunnels, over low pillows, and around stationary objects. These obstacle courses can be created, rearranged, and dismantled as needed.
- Help toddlers become aware of how close they are to other children. When they are too close to another child or, in some cases, almost on top of another child, use words and redirection to help them move and give the other child some space. "You are too close to Darnell. He can't move around. Come and sit here." (Indicate where the child should sit.)
- If two children are often too close to each other, try sitting on the floor with them with your legs out in front of you. Have one child on one side of you and the other child on the other side. The children are near each other, but you are helping to organize the space by the placement of your legs.
- If a child is really struggling with space issues, have him sit at the end of a table rather than in the middle with other children on each side. Another strategy is to let him use a toy that defines his space for him, such as a toy car he can sit in. Of course, you'll have to have other toy cars for some of the other children.

EMERGING AUTONOMY

Toddlers need many opportunities to feel powerful and competent while still feeling and being safe. You can help foster the child's sense of having power by structuring choices—letting the child make a choice and then respecting that choice. Toddlers do best with a simple choice between two alternatives, both of which are acceptable. For example, you can offer the toddler the choice between fingerpainting or using brushes to paint, or between putting the napkin on the table first or the cup on the table first. When the toddler makes the choice, reinforce the power of choosing and support the choice by commenting, "You decided to put the napkin on first." Then make sure you let the child follow through. Try to provide as many opportunities for choosing as possible because so often you must place limits on toddlers' behavior to keep them safe.

EXPRESSIVE LANGUAGE DEVELOPMENT

- Always respond to children's verbal communications, including babbling, jabbering, words, and phrases. This lets them understand that verbal communication is valuable.
- Name objects, materials, and people. Children's brains love to make connections, and when two things happen at the same time, a connection is made. So when you hand a child a spoon and say, "Here's your spoon," the child makes the connection between the object and its name. This helps children develop vocabulary to describe what they want, which can reduce their frustration at not being able to express themselves. It also gives them a way of communicating other than biting.
- Put words with actions. Describe what you are doing and what the children are doing. "You put the car on top of the table. You're using your hand to make it go fast."
- Have conversations with children. Listen to what they are saying. Follow their lead, add some more information, or ask a question, then wait for the child to continue the conversation. These conversations help to extend children's language. Children are more likely to participate in such conversations and speak more than when adults initiate or dominate conversations.

NEED FOR ATTENTION

If you think a child is biting to get attention, try giving him lots of attention before he resorts to biting. Give attention freely and lavishly; don't make the child wait, ask for, or earn it. Often the child who needs positive attention the most is the one we are least likely to give it to. Make an effort to notice and comment on all the child's acceptable behaviors—being curious, helping, creating, and so forth. In this way you can teach the child who had been biting that other, more positive behaviors are even more likely to get your attention.

HOLDING ON AND LETTING GO

- Give the toddler lots of opportunities to practice physical holding on and letting go. This can be in the form of two favorite toddler activities, "pick up little things and put them into containers" and "pick up, carry around, and dump." Both give the child the opportunity to practice and enjoy holding on and letting go.

- Work on emotional "letting go" as well. Help toddlers who are having a difficult time with separations by telling them, for example, "You're so sad when your daddy has to go. It's hard for you when Daddy leaves. He will go to work, and then he will come back after we play outside."
- Children who are having trouble holding on and letting go may not be able to control and "let go" of urine or feces, so hold off on toilet learning.

Strategies and Techniques Related to Expressing Feelings

Chapter 1 listed the common feelings that get expressed through biting, including frustration and anger, tension, anxiety, and excitement. Here are some strategies and techniques for dealing with each.

FRUSTRATION AND ANGER

- Capitalize on toddlers' desire to imitate by expressing your own frustration and anger in words. Teach the child to say an emphatic "No!" or "Stop it!" to another child who is trying to take a toy or book away from him. Encourage children to say, "I don't like it when . . ." or "I am so mad when . . ." Being able to express feelings with heartfelt words may prevent children from expressing those feelings with their teeth.
- Learn to recognize signs of frustration in the child. When you see him begin to get frustrated, use redirection to help him out of the situation. For example, a six-piece puzzle may be too difficult for him. Be prepared to redirect him to a puzzle with three pieces so he can experience success instead of frustration.

TENSION

- Observe the child so you will recognize signs of mounting tension.
- Help to relieve tension in the child's mouth and jaw by gently massaging the joint where the jaw meets the skull (just in front of the ear) with circular motions. But don't just swoop down and begin manipulating the face of a child who is already tense. To be more respectful and effective, approach the child from the front and make eye contact. Begin by gently tracing circles on the back of her hand while using a soft, rhythmic voice to say, "I'm making little circles on your hand." Then gradually move up to the arm while saying, "I'm making little circles on your arm." Work up to the child's shoulders. "I'm making little circles on your shoulder." Finally, move your fingers to the spot you want to massage in front of the ear. "I'm making little circles by your ear." Massage is so

calming that you may want to do it regularly to get the children in your program used to it. Then when you need to use it to relieve the tension that may be a factor in biting, children will be more likely to accept it.

- Step in to redirect when a child is getting into a potentially tense situation. For example, a child may try to get into a private space that another child is already occupying. If you can help him find another space or another way of meeting his need for privacy, he is less likely to bite.
- Provide more gross-motor activities—such as moving the arms, legs, and torso to music—to relieve tension.
- Try going outside more often to relieve the tension associated with being in confined spaces.

ANXIETY

- Use your own observations and information from the child's parents to understand why the child may be anxious or what she may be worried about. Use reassuring language with the child. "I'm going to be right here when you need me."
- Provide a calm atmosphere by playing soothing music and giving the child one-on-one attention during the day.
- Make sure there is a place for the child to go to get away from the pressures of the group. This might be a quiet corner with soft pillows or a "house" made out of a big cardboard box and just big enough for one.
- Help the child calm herself by allowing her to suck a pacifier or her thumb (if she already does this) or by using a comfort object such as a favorite blanket from home.
- Give the child plenty of time to eat, make transitions, use the toilet, and so on to reduce feelings of pressure.
- Soothe the child at naptime with back rubs and songs.

EXCITEMENT

- Encourage toddlers to develop a variety of physical (nonbiting) expressions of excitement. For example, have them clap happily, jump up and down, dance around, and yell "Yay!" Do this with them when the occasion calls for excitement.
- Be aware that some children have intense reactions to almost everything. This is part of their inborn temperament, and you will notice that these children seem to react more quickly and with more vigor than other children. When they are excited, this inborn tendency to react intensely may result in biting. During moments

of great excitement, you may want to position yourself near them to direct their excitement to an appropriate action.

Shadowing: A Last-Ditch Technique

When you have exhausted all other possibilities, you may want to try having someone shadow the child who is biting. Shadowing involves having one staff person stay with the child, positioning herself where she can always intercept a bite. Because one staff person must be devoted to watching and staying with just one child, shadowing is often difficult for programs to do. Shadowing requires intense vigilance, but it often works. The staff person shadowing the child is usually able to redirect the child before biting occurs, showing the child different, more acceptable behavior. This means that instead of biting, the child is going through the day *not* biting, and this can become his new behavior.

Parents often ask that programs shadow children who are biting as one of the first techniques to try because it seems like the most logical intervention. However, a carefully crafted, appropriate plan will ultimately work better because it will address the reasons for the biting. This is especially true if there are factors in the child care environment that are contributing to biting. Shadowing might stop a child from biting in the moment, but if the difficult environmental factors are still in place, the child is almost sure to bite again after the shadowing stops. You should try a complete plan of other strategies for several weeks, adjusting as needed, before resorting to shadowing. Remember that you are looking for improvement, not perfection. If the biting diminishes, stick with your plan. Changes are stressful for children, and giving up on your plan when it is working can bring biting back.

A less intensive version of shadowing can be used successfully when one child repeatedly bites the same child. Try bringing the two children together for very closely supervised play—perhaps sensory play at a sand or water table. Have an adult place herself between the children and supervise, interacting with both children and standing ready to make an intervention if the situation warrants it. This gives both children the opportunity to experience bite-free interaction. Further, it allows the child who has been biting to get positive attention for positive interactions.

Implement the Plan

Decide on a length of time to try the plan, allow enough time to implement the changes, and follow them consistently. Usually at least a week or two is needed before you can expect to see significant changes in the children. Share your written plan with the parents of all the children in the program. (See page 72 for a sample letter that illustrates how to do this effectively.)

Then begin the trial period. The plan will need to be followed consistently in order to work. If you plan to offer the water table every day, but you only manage to get it open once or twice during the week, you probably haven't made a big enough change to affect the biting. This doesn't mean that the change didn't work—you haven't really made the change yet. Ask your administrator for support and encouragement during this time. And don't forget to keep observing carefully. You may discover new information about the child who is biting, the children who are being bitten, or the program. New information can help you revise or fine-tune your plan so it keeps working.

Finally, evaluate your progress. At the end of the specified trial period, determine whether the biting has decreased. If it has, celebrate your success and keep going. Don't measure your success by whether the biting has stopped completely; that's probably not a realistic short-term goal. If the number of attempted and actual bites has decreased, the plan is working. The biting will continue to decrease over time if you keep observing children and meeting their needs, and eventually it will stop completely.

If the biting hasn't decreased at all, you will need to modify your plan or create a new one. To do that, you will have to review your observations during the trial period and think about what seemed to work and why, as well as what didn't work and why. You will have to think about what parts of the plan you were able to implement and what you didn't do quite the way you thought you would. Then modify your plan, taking these insights into account. It's a good idea not to change your strategies completely from one week to the next; rather, keep your plan pretty much the same and fine-tune it to make it work better for you and for the children.

Share Your Plan with Parents

Parents need to know what you are doing about ongoing biting. Sharing your plan openly in a letter demonstrates to parents your willingness to admit a problem exists and shows them you know what you are going to do to address ongoing biting. This encourages them to have confidence in the program.

Appendix A contains a sample letter to parents explaining your plan to address ongoing biting. This sample deals with a hypothetical biting situation. It is designed to help you formulate your own letter based on your plan for dealing with ongoing biting in your program.

Helping the Child Who Is Being Bitten Repeatedly

With so much attention focused on the child who is biting, it is easy to forget that the child who is being bitten may also need help. Any time a child is bitten, we need to provide first aid, comfort, support, and reassurance. But when we notice a particular child is being bitten again and again, that child may need more help from us. We don't want children to feel helpless, and we don't want children to become comfortable in the role of victim. Learning to stand up for themselves is an important social and emotional goal for young children. We also want to help the child who is being bitten repeatedly because that child may respond by biting in return.

First, let the child know that it is all right to be mad (or frightened or worried) when someone bites him. You may have to tell him, "You don't like it when Mary bites you. She hurt you."

Second, help children learn to say no when another child is hurting them. This language may range from a simple, emphatic "No!" or "Stop!" to longer phrases such as "Don't bite me." Model the words and tone for children to use. It will be much easier for them to learn to stand up for themselves if they can start by imitating your words and tone instead of trying to come up with their own. This also gives you another possibility for preventing a bite: when you hear children using their new words, respond quickly, and you may be able to help them solve a problem before one of them gets bitten. Specific suggestions for helping children learn to stand up for themselves are covered in the section called "Helping the Child Who Was Bitten" on pages 18–19 in chapter 2.

As with any technique or strategy, you need to base your actions on observations. If you are observing a child who is being bitten a great deal, you may discover that something the child is doing is resulting in her being bitten. An example might be a girl grabbing a toy right out of the hands of a boy, who then bites her. You don't want the boy to bite, and you don't want the girl to be bitten. At the same time, you don't want the girl to take the toy away from the boy. In this case, you need to redirect the girl toward a different toy and help her begin to understand that she may not grab a toy away from someone else. Both children need to learn different behavior.

This is also an opportunity to give the child who is being bitten some advice. This advice falls into the category of cause and effect.

When you grab his toys away from him, he bites you. When you want a toy that someone else has, let me help you ask for it.

When you get so close to Mariah, she bites you. Mariah doesn't want anyone to get so close to her. You can get really close to me. Then we can go to Mariah together.

For in-depth examples of observation techniques and planning, see appendix B.

Working with Parents and Other Community Members

Biting in child care programs can strain even the best relationships between parents and programs. Child Care Solutions has found that parents want two things when it comes to biting:

- They want programs and providers to take it as seriously as they do.
- They want the biting to stop.

Caregivers and Parents Have Different Perspectives

Caregivers and directors in child care programs serving toddlers often claim that "parents just don't understand about biting." In one sense, this is true. They don't understand biting the same way caregivers understand it, and that's not surprising. Experienced caregivers and directors most likely have dealt with many biting incidents in the course of their work with toddlers. They have probably read books and articles and attended training related to biting. The sheer amount of biting they deal with shapes their understanding of biting. On the other hand, parents may have very little experience with biting because they do not interact with the number of toddlers that caregivers do year after year. It is almost guaranteed that parents will look at biting differently than caregivers do. The chart below presents some of these differences very clearly:

When it comes to biting, caregivers	When it comes to biting, parents
are not surprised when toddlers bite;	are very surprised when toddlers bite—sometimes even shocked;
know that biting is not unusual behavior for toddlers and doesn't necessarily indicate something is seriously wrong;	assume something must be terribly wrong either with the child or with the program when toddlers bite;
know toddlers bite for many reasons;	may see toddler biting as a deliberate act of aggression;
know it may take some time before the biting stops;	believe that biting can be stopped quickly and easily;
know they can't guarantee there will be no biting.	believe biting can be "guaranteed against."

I developed this chart after conversations with many parents and caregivers during conflicts over toddler biting. In talking with parents, I began to identify some common themes in their responses to biting and in their comments and questions about the child care programs. I listed these themes and shared them with toddler caregivers in workshops. In workshop after workshop, caregivers recognized the themes and had experienced parents' responses reflecting those themes. These responses do not necessarily apply to every parent, but in conflicts about biting, they are often present.

It is essential that caregivers and directors understand their difference in perspective; it is equally important that they *acknowledge* parents' perspective on biting. They do not have to agree with it, but they must accept that this is the way parents look at biting. Since our actions are based on our particular perspective, when we understand parents' beliefs about biting, we are better able to understand the depth of their feelings and the certainty of their convictions about biting. We can also understand their reactions, suggestions, and demands. Then we can use these insights to determine what we must do to be effective with parents when toddlers are biting.

While we must acknowledge the parents' perspective, we cannot base our approach to biting on it. Our approach to biting must be based on our knowledge of why children bite and of developmentally appropriate practices to help reduce the biting. Nevertheless, we can use our knowledge and understanding of the parents' perspective to create effective approaches to *parents*.

Parents' Common Reactions

The following are three common parents' reactions to providers and to biting situations in their children's child care programs.

Parents often say their concerns are being taken lightly. We have found that parents are upset when programs calmly explain biting in terms of "normal toddler development." For parents, saying that something is normal implies that it is to be expected and tolerated. This is upsetting for parents because biting is not something *they* expected, and they most certainly do not want to tolerate anything that hurts their children.

Parents often feel that the teachers and the director don't care that their children were bitten. Teachers who have cared for toddlers for many years have probably dealt with hundreds of biting incidents. Over the years they have likely developed effective techniques to address biting and may also have worked hard to put everything they have learned about biting into explanations and information for parents. Sometimes the very words they have carefully chosen to inform and reassure parents may be interpreted by parents as "not taking the biting seriously." When caregivers talk with parents about biting, they must make sure to express genuine regret about it and recognize and acknowledge parents' shock, pain, and (if it is present) outrage.

Parents often report that when biting becomes an ongoing problem, teachers and directors tell them they're taking care of it but offer no specific information on how. When parents don't see any changes in either the program or the amount of biting, they suspect nothing is being done. Then they feel the program is either unable or unwilling to address the biting. When parents lose confidence in the program, they may resort to threats of taking their children out of it or demands that children who bite be expelled. When parents know that specific steps are being taken to address the biting, they are much more likely to be supportive.

What Can Parents Reasonably Expect of Programs?

Here is a list of what parents can reasonably expect from their child's program when it comes to biting. Use it as a quick checklist to assess if you are doing everything you can to support and reassure parents when biting is an issue in your program.

Parents can reasonably expect that a good child care program will

- put children's safety first and provide appropriate first aid as well as comfort, support, and advice to any child who is bitten;
- provide appropriate programming for their toddlers, thus reducing the likelihood of biting;
- help children who are biting for any reason to learn not to bite;
- give parents current information or resources on biting;
- ensure that teachers have adequate knowledge and training to deal appropriately and effectively with biting;
- take parents' concerns seriously and treat parents with understanding and respect;
- tell parents what specific steps are being taken to address biting and explain the reasons for those steps;
- respond to their questions, concerns, and suggestions—even when the response to their suggestions is "no";
- be willing to schedule parent-teacher conferences about biting at a time when parents can come;
- keep their child's identity confidential if he or she bites to avoid labeling or confrontations with other families that will slow the process of learning not to bite.

Appendix A contains a version of this list incorporated into a letter to parents. You can use a letter like this to let parents know what they can expect from your program, and parents can use it as a checklist to evaluate the way your program handles an actual biting episode. You can ask parents to check whether or not you did the things you said you would do. This may help focus parents' attention on program responses that are appropriate rather than on inappropriate responses they may suggest.

Note that the last item in the letter refers to keeping *their* child's identity confidential if she or he bites. We have used this wording to help parents identify with the child who is biting. Some parents feel that the staff is withholding information from them when they keep a child's name confidential. It's important to help parents understand why confidentiality is necessary in order to stop the biting and why confidentiality is a positive thing. You can also use the phrasing in the list above in your letter to parents.

Saying No: When You Can't Give Parents What They Want

Sometimes parents ask for something we cannot or are not willing to give them. Parents often call Child Care Solutions to say that all they want is a guarantee that their child will not be bitten, and they truly believe that good programs should be able to give them that. After all, "I pay good money for that child care; they should at least be able to make sure no one bites my child."

While we acknowledge that such a guarantee would be wonderful, we can't give it because we truthfully can't make that promise to parents. Child Care Solutions gently tells parents that any program offering such a guarantee is lying to them, fooling itself, or willing to do things to children that they don't even want to imagine.

Parents may ask programs to

- keep "the biter" away from their child;
- give them the name of the child who is biting their son or daughter;
- kick out the child who is biting;
- punish the biting child by withholding snacks or activities;
- demand that "the biter" be tested for HIV/AIDS and/or hepatitis;
- allow them to handle the biting situation themselves by punishing the other child's parents;
- allow them to discipline the child who bit their son or daughter;
- suspend the child who bit for a few weeks to "break the biting cycle."

Sometimes these suggestions and demands catch us off guard because, at least to us, they are so obviously the wrong thing to do. But we must take into consideration the emotional nature of parents' responses to biting. In the heat of the moment, parents may want to punish the child who bit or the child's parents. Sometimes their demands are an attempt to impress on us just how serious this biting is. This is especially the case when parents demand that the child who bit be tested for HIV/AIDS. Parents may also want to force something on the child or her parents just as the bite was forced on their child.

Parents want decisive action, and they are more than willing to give us suggestions. Teachers need to be responsive and respectful even when they say no to inappropriate suggestions. This is not easy, but it is a child care provider's responsibility. Here are some examples of responses that respect and recognize the perspective of the parent but still do not comply with their suggestion or demand.

You would like to have a child who is biting stay home for a few weeks so he can have some "bite-free" time and maybe break the biting cycle. And the child may indeed not bite during the weeks he would be out of the program. But when he came back, if nothing had changed here or if he hadn't learned different behavior, he would just start biting again. I want us to spend our energy and time improving our program and helping him learn different behavior.

Seeing that bite on your child must be so frightening. It looks so awful. Now you're worried about AIDS because of the saliva and broken skin. We worried about biting and AIDS, too, so we checked to see whether AIDS is spread by biting. We found out that it isn't. I can give you a copy of that information. This may take care of that worry, but biting is still very upsetting. See pages 70–71 for information on HIV/AIDS.

You're so angry that your child was bitten, and you want me to let you punish the child who bit her. But this is something I am not willing to do. It might make you feel better, but it would not help the child learn different behavior. This is not easy for me to say, because I like to be able to give parents what they want. I would like to tell you what we have decided to do about the biting. (This is a good lead-in to sharing the plan you have developed.)

Parents may also try to put pressure on caregivers to break confidentiality and tell them the name of the child who is biting. They may say they have other ways of finding out, so the caregiver might as well tell them. It is quite likely they may find out who bit their child because their child may be able to tell them. It is difficult to respond when a parent says, "You might as well tell me, because I'm going to find out anyway." Here is a response that recognizes the parent may indeed learn the name of the child who bit from someone else and that helps the caregiver maintain professionalism:

You might hear who bit your child from someone else, but you will not hear it from me. I work hard to maintain confidentiality. I would not give out the name of your child, and I won't give out the name of another child. You can count on me to work very hard at solving the biting situation, and you can count on me to keep confidentiality.

Responding to Well-Intentioned Bad Advice

Over the years, members of the Task Force on Biting had received a great deal of advice from parents and others on how to handle biting. Some of these suggestions have been sound, but many have been ineffective, some impossible, and a few actually cruel. If you care for toddlers, you have probably encountered (or will encounter) these or similar suggestions when biting incidents occur:

- Forcing something into the child's mouth (people have suggested vinegar, lemon juice, pepper, soap, even cigarette butts)

- Punishing the child at home that evening
- Bribing the child not to bite
- Biting the child back
- Having the other child bite back
- Spanking the child
- Making the child go to the director's office
- Popping the child under the chin after biting
- Keeping the child away from other children or away from one child in particular

Occasionally the suggestions are offered out of a desperate desire to do *something*. More often the advice is well-intentioned, and people offer it because they think it will work. They may even share an anecdote to prove their point. More than once a parent has said, "Well, my child bit one time. I bit her back, and let me tell you, she never bit again!" This may be true, but it doesn't necessarily mean that the child stopped biting because the parent bit her back. It also does not mean that biting children back will stop them from biting in other situations. We have heard from parents who bit their children back and ended up with furious toddlers on a biting rampage.

In order to respond effectively to parents who make these suggestions, you need to know why these are inappropriate responses to biting. Acknowledging the perspective of the person offering the advice is the first step to an effective response. Being able to begin your response in a sincere tone with something such as, "I know it sounds like that might stop the biting . . ." makes it much more likely that the rest of your response will be taken seriously. Let's take a look at these suggestions one by one to see why they don't work, and why no good program would ever use them.

Forcing something into the child's mouth. This may be suggested as an effective punishment. The reasoning behind the technique is that toddlers will stop biting to stop the unpleasant tastes being forced into their mouths or will associate biting with the unpleasant experience and therefore stop. Good programs and providers, however, do not guide or correct children's behavior in ways that hurt or frighten the child. Toddlers who have things forced into their mouths will most likely be confused, scared, or furious. They will also become distrustful of the adults who did it. This is a prescription to encourage biting, not stop it.

Punishing the child at home. Most parents feel they should do something to address the biting. They don't want their children to bite, and they feel they need to have some kind of response. Since they weren't at the scene of the biting when it occurred, they try to punish the child later at home. This may make the parent feel better, but it's ineffective because the child won't connect the punishment to the biting.

Bribing the child not to bite. As with punishment, parents usually try bribery because they want to do *something* to stop the biting. And it's important for teachers to understand that parents may really believe it will work. Since adults are able to understand the concept of being rewarded for something they do (or don't do), it is tempting to think that toddlers understand this as well. But toddlers don't make the connection between the action and the promised reward and don't make decisions about behavior based on delayed rewards. If a toddler does remember anything about the statement, "If you don't bite, I'll give you a sticker [or some other special treat]," it is likely to be the reward. Toddlers have been known to run to their parents at the end of a day punctuated by biting to excitedly await the promised reward. When parents find out that the child has bitten several times that day, they express surprise that their child still expects the reward.

Biting the child back. This seems to be the prevailing advice given by parents as a surefire way to get toddlers to stop biting. The reasoning is that if toddlers experience the pain of biting, they'll stop biting others. This technique is usually ineffective because what toddlers actually experience is an adult biting them for no reason that the toddler can figure out. Furthermore, biting back is ineffective because children learn behavior that adults model for them. If adults bite, children will learn to bite from them. If adults bite children, children learn it's okay to bite if you're bigger, stronger, or in the right. This will not stop them from biting.

Finally, the most damaging aspect of biting back is the effect it has on children's trust and sense of security with staff in a child care program. Children need to know they can trust their caregivers and they are safe at child care and at home, which is not true if caregivers bite them. Children who don't feel secure are more likely to bite.

Having the other child bite back. This is a variation on having the adult bite the child back and is ineffective for the same reasons. In this case, you are actually teaching children to bite by allowing (or perhaps even insisting) that a child bite! This technique is cruel to both children.

Spanking the child. This is yet another technique involving physical punishment to address biting. It is ineffective and damaging for the same reasons cited in the section on biting the child back. In addition, most states do not permit corporal punishment in child care centers.

Making the child go to the director's office. This technique has actually been written into the plan of some child care programs, often to show the parents that something is being done about the biting. While it does remove the child from the room, it does nothing to address the reason the child is biting or to guide the child in learning other behavior. When the child returns to the room, nothing has changed, including the biting.

Popping the child under the chin after biting. Apparently this is sometimes used to train puppies not to bite. It may be suggested on the basis of "If it works with puppies, it should work with kids." Children, however, need to learn how not to bite, and this technique doesn't help them. In addition, it is likely to frighten, startle, or hurt the child, and damage his sense of trust and security in the child care program. These results are likely to cause more biting. Can anyone imagine caregivers hitting toddlers on the nose with a rolled-up newspaper every time they have an accident while they are learning to use the toilet?

Keeping the child away from other children or from one other child in particular. This is a seemingly commonsense approach to keeping a particular child safe. The problem is that it is almost impossible to limit toddlers to certain areas of the room or to make particular children "off limits." In addition, there may be several biting patterns going on, and caregivers could not possibly keep straight who was not supposed to play with whom.

From a philosophical viewpoint, keeping children apart so they can't interact is the complete opposite of what we are trying to facilitate. If we want children to learn to interact without biting, they need the opportunity to play together. When biting occurs, the task of teaching children how to be with one another becomes more difficult, which highlights the need to do it well. When there seems to be a recurring pattern of one child choosing a particular child to bite, caregivers need to increase their supervision of those particular children, but caregivers can't be expected to keep the children apart.

When responding to inappropriate suggestions, some toddler caregivers like to use a standard phrase such as, "Oh, we're not allowed to do that in our program," or "It's against state regulations." This sounds as though they agree that the suggestion is a good one and would try it if it weren't for the rules and regulations. It's tempting to say something like this because it puts you on the parents' side for the moment. It looks as though you agree, and you are united with parents against "the program" or "the state." This approach may seem easier than giving parents the bad news that you don't agree with them and possibly getting into an argument.

Unfortunately, siding with parents in this manner usually backfires, because it's not really honest. If you helped to create the program's plan to address the biting, and you understand why a parent's suggestion would not work, giving parents the impression that you agree with them is not telling the truth. It gives parents the idea that even the staff disagree on what to do about the biting. This is confusing for parents, who then don't know whom to believe or what is right for their children. Dishonesty also can make parents feel as though staff are not willing to take responsibility for the program's decisions. This can weaken parents' confidence in the program, making it harder for them to trust that staff are really doing the best they can to stop the biting. In the end, your job becomes harder because parents who don't feel they can trust the program will give you much less support when you need it.

If you don't feel that you can explain the reasons adequately, or if you are afraid of a confrontation, it's okay to suggest that a parent talk with the director. You can say something such as, "I know it sounds like that would work, but it really doesn't. This is hard for me to explain, and Jennifer can talk about it much more clearly than I can." Let Jennifer know you have referred the parents to her, and then work on developing explanations in your own words so you will be able to share them directly with parents in the future.

Sometimes it's true that caregivers don't agree with the plan that has been made and would like to use one of the methods outlined above to address the biting. If this is the case, it's important to take a look at why you are working in a program that has a philosophy so different from yours. It's not okay to tell parents you disagree with the program's policies, because it's not fair to put parents in the middle of a disagreement between you and the rest of the staff. As an employee in a child care center, you must realize and accept your responsibility to carry out the philosophy, policies, and procedures of the center. You may need to think about whether it would be better for you to work in a program whose philosophy better matches your own. At the same time, consider the reasons the techniques listed above are inappropriate. The bottom line is that they don't work in the long run and they damage children. It is never okay for a child care program to use strategies that damage children to address a problem.

Helping the Parents of the Child Who Is Biting

When parents learn their child has bitten another child, their reaction can range from feelings of shock and guilt to accusations that the program is doing something wrong. It is important to work closely with parents so you and they can share information that may affect the biting. You will also want to let parents know what you are observing in the program and what responses you are trying.

Parents whose child was bitten and those whose child did the biting often say they felt more helpless when their child was the one who bit. You may need to offer as much support to these parents as you do to their children.

Overall, you want to make sure that you and the parents are working together to end the biting, even though much of the specific work will be done in your program, because that is where the biting is occurring. If the biting is also occurring at home, you will want to work with parents to discover a likely cause and then develop a plan to work with the child consistently at child care and at home.

Parents may ask how they can help at home. Here are some suggestions:

- If you have a good idea of why you believe the child is biting, share the strategies and techniques related to those reasons with parents. They may be able to work on some at home. (Strategies and techniques are found on pages 33–40 in chapter 3.)
- If the parents are doing the innocent "play" biting described under "Imitation" on pages 9–10 in chapter 1, encourage them to replace it with some other affectionate behavior until the child is a little older.
- Help parents learn the importance of expressing disapproval for biting if the child bites at home. You may give them suggestions on doing this effectively, including appropriate tone of voice and wording. Help them understand that this does not mean lecturing, going off on a tirade, or punishing the child.
- Encourage parents to help their toddler develop language skills and to model appropriate ways to express feelings as well as caring and empathetic behavior.

Since many parents want to suggest punishments, you need to be prepared to explain just how valuable these actions will be for their child. Parents may imply that the fault lies with you or the program because their child "doesn't bite at home." Often this is the case, because many of the reasons toddlers bite are related to being around more people. Instead of reacting defensively, acknowledge that this may indeed be true and that the reasons their child is biting may be related to the group setting and the frustration that sometimes comes with it for toddlers.

Helping the Parents of the Child Who Is Being Bitten

Many programs report that this is one of the toughest jobs they have. Most parents react very strongly to biting. You can't assume that parents won't be furious with you if their child is bitten simply because you have previously had a good relationship with them. Even the most understanding, reasonable, knowledgeable parents can't help feeling a lump in their throat and a rising level of righteous rage when they see bite wounds on their toddlers. Sometimes it seems toddlers are bitten on the face more than any other part of the body; such bites appear not only painful but also disfiguring.

You need to recognize that the first response many parents have to biting is, "Where were you when this happened?" You may feel attacked, but such a question should not be entirely unexpected. Parents weren't there to protect their child, and to them it looks as if you weren't either. This is probably not the time to explain how very quickly toddlers can bite. Try responding with genuine regret as you tell them, "I wasn't where I could have stopped the bite. I feel terrible. I don't want any of the children to get bitten."

Here are some keys to an effective conversation with the parents of the child who was bitten:

- Acknowledge and respect the parents' feelings and the depth of those feelings.
- Tell them how you will help keep their child safe. This might include both increasing supervision and helping the child learn to stand up for herself. This helps the parent understand that you're not expecting the child to be responsible for her own safety, but you also do not want her to see herself as a victim.
- Tell them what you are doing to teach the child who bit not to bite anymore.

At this point parents are likely to give suggestions, make demands, or issue ultimatums that you cannot accept. Be prepared for your efforts to go unappreciated by parents until the biting stops. You may be trying your very best, but parents are looking for results—often quick results. You can't stop the biting cycle as fast as they would like, which means you need to use all of your skills in working with families. Look to your program administrator for support.

Working with Parents of Other Children in the Program

When you're working with parents during biting episodes, most of your efforts will likely go toward the parents of the children directly involved. Parents of other children in the program, however, are almost certainly aware of what is happening and may also need some information and reassurance. There are several ways you can help these parents.

First, make sure they know what you are doing to address the biting, and ask them to bring questions they have directly to you. Parents who feel they can get information and answers from you will be less likely to go to other parents to find out what they want to know. If you have developed a plan to deal with ongoing biting, all parents should have a copy of that plan and updates as the plan proceeds.

Second, tell them what you are doing to protect children from biting. This is especially important for parents of the youngest children in the group. These children may not be able to talk or get around as easily as older children, so parents may worry that these children will be easy targets for others who are biting. Let parents know you will tell them of any reactions their child may have to the biting in the room. Reassure them that you will comfort their child if he is upset by the biting. Ask them to share with you any reactions they notice in their child that they think may be related to the biting.

Finally, give them specific suggestions they can use at home with their own children. Advise them to follow their child's lead. If their child does not talk about the biting, they shouldn't pump the child for information. If their child tells them that a particular toddler is biting in their room, the parent can say, "I don't like biting, and Miss Nancy doesn't like biting. Miss Nancy will tell Adam, 'No biting!'"

If their child expresses concern that someone might bite him, parents can tell their child, "I don't want anyone to bite you. You can tell Adam, 'No biting!'" If the child seems quite worried, the parent can add, "We'll tell Miss Nancy that you're worried, and she will help you."

Parents can also help their child learn words that label feelings, and they can model helping, empathetic behaviors for their child to imitate. Toddlers who can express their feelings and have experience with helping and empathy may be less likely to become participants in biting episodes; this may help reduce ongoing biting.

While these suggestions do not guarantee that children will never be bitten, they do help parents respond in a way that is reassuring and appropriate to their toddlers.

Sharing Success

You may want to have caregivers count and record the number of bites they intercept and prevent. This can help parents and staff alike recognize how their efforts are helping reduce the number of bites, and it can be especially useful if you have parents who are keeping their own running tally of the number of bites in your program. Keeping track of "saves" is a familiar practice; it is used in both hockey and soccer. Of course, the number of "saves" may not matter as much to parents as the number of bites, and you can't very well say, "Yeah, there were two bites today. But we had five saves, so it's okay." It's much more effective to say, "We did have two bites today, and that was upsetting. We're glad, though, that there were five other bites we were able to see coming and stop before they happened." When people are counting, it's good to be able to recognize and acknowledge that "saves" count too. (Use this suggestion cautiously with parents, though. You don't want to antagonize them by focusing more on saves than on what is being done to stop the biting.)

When the Outside Community Is Aware of the Biting

Parents are not the only adults who have an interest in biting episodes at your program. You may occasionally find that the entire community seems to know that you have "a biting problem." Suddenly people who don't even have children in your program are talking about it at the grocery store, at work, and at community gatherings. It may seem that everyone is an expert on biting, giving opinions or passing judgment on your program and making pronouncements along the lines of "If *I* were in charge, I wouldn't allow biting in the first place—let me tell you!"

This will most likely happen when parents talk to their friends and family about the biting and how the child care program is handling it. Of course, the people who are the most dissatisfied seem to talk the most. This can certainly hurt the reputation of your program and can also discourage staff. You can hardly issue a general gag order concerning the biting. Telling people they are forbidden to talk about what is happening will certainly backfire and result in even less confidence in the program. It is likely to ensure that there will be even more negative comments about the program.

What you *can* do is try to create the message you *do* want the community to hear and then use every opportunity to get that message out. Your message needs to be genuine, positive, and engaging. It must also be true; that is, it must reflect what you really do.

Here is such a message: "Whenever we face challenges at the ABC Early Childhood Program, we work on them in ways that are appropriate for children, families, and staff. And we are willing to take the time to do it well." This message should be incorporated into the public relations work you do with the community. Do not wait for negative events or publicity and then issue defensive statements. Give the community an exciting, positive picture of your program on a regular basis. Write articles for community publications about what the children are doing in your program, and include pictures. Write informative articles for parents about child development. As you tell the community about your program, work in the message about how you handle problems. You can also include this message in letters, memos, and newsletters to families. Post it on bulletin boards. Put it in the parents' handbook. Then, when people in the community ask questions or make comments about the "terrible biting" in the program, you can encourage staff to use your program's message in their response.

Staff Members Working Together

During episodes of ongoing biting, parents are not the only adults who are under stress and perhaps feeling frustrated. The caregivers in the room also feel the pressure, because they are the ones who are trying to carry out the program, care for the toddlers, work with the parents, and stem the biting. To deal with biting effectively, toddler caregivers need information about biting, support from the administrator and other staff, resources to carry out a plan, and relief when necessary.

This book provides the information toddler caregivers need to understand biting and to choose responses that are likely to work. When biting becomes a repeated problem, they may need help from their administrator and other staff to develop a plan. Other teachers can help by serving as "fresh eyes" to observe the toddler room for program components that may be contributing to the biting. This is an important part of developing a plan to address ongoing biting, because caregivers who are in the room every day may not be able to see problems in the program.

Once a plan has been developed, toddler caregivers will certainly need the help and support of the program administrator and other teachers to implement it. The plan may call for a change in the room arrangement or the daily schedule, different or less equipment, additional materials, or even additional staff. Caregivers in the toddler program need to know how to request the help (or permission) they need to make these changes. They may need some physical help from other teachers to rearrange the room or remove equipment. If part of the plan involves additional staff, toddler caregivers need to know that the staff member joining them sees this assignment as a problem-solving opportunity rather than a punishment.

Toddler caregivers need to know that they can count on their coworkers not only for help with tasks but also for moral support as they take on biting. Without going into great detail, the program administrator should let all staff know what is happening. This can be as simple a statement as "Room

3 is working hard to deal with a rash of biting. They have developed a plan they will be trying over the next two weeks, and they need support from all of us. Please see me if you would like to help."

Other staff can help by asking how the plan is progressing and offering to listen with a sympathetic ear. They can also help by knowing how to respond to parents who complain to them about the biting and how it's being handled. It is quite likely that parents of toddlers in the room with the biting problem also have older children in the program. Some parents may try to draw the teachers of their older children into a discussion of the biting. This is the time for those teachers to support their colleagues in the toddler room by stating their confidence in the toddler caregivers and the plan they developed. They should direct the parents to speak directly with the teachers in the toddler room or with the program administrator. If other staff have concerns about how the biting is being handled, they owe it to the program to take those concerns to the administrator directly and privately.

Caregivers who are doing the hard work of addressing biting need to know where they can express their frustration and how they can get some relief from time to time. This is more difficult than it may seem. Stressed caregivers cannot just leave the room and take a break whenever they feel like it, because toddlers must be supervised and ratios must be maintained. Other staff cannot just trot in and out of the room all day to provide breaks; toddlers thrive on consistency and often fall apart when there are too many changes.

Programs may have to look for creative solutions to the problem of giving breaks to teachers stressed out by the biting. Is there any period during which having other staff in the room might be minimally disruptive to toddlers? For example, other teachers or a floater might be able to fill in for short periods during naptime. Administrators might use this break time to meet with caregivers and give them an opportunity to talk about how they are feeling, how the plan is working, and what additional help they need. Administrators can also provide some relief by being in the classroom to talk with parents at pickup time, which can be an overwhelming time of the day for caregivers.

Finally, if everybody in the program knows about the biting problems in the toddler room, then everybody ought to be told whenever there is measurable success. Administrators should publicize the good news, and other staff should offer sincere congratulations.

The Role of the Program Administrator

The program administrator plays a crucial role in addressing biting. She develops policies, supports staff, conducts staff development, communicates with parents, and sets the tone for the program. These are all crucial when a program is struggling with biting. During a biting episode, the administrator has a number of responsibilities, including

- making sure program policies related to biting are being followed;
- supporting teachers, giving them suggestions, and allowing them to vent their frustrations in private;
- providing appropriate staff development on biting;
- knowing where to find additional information, authorities, and technical assistance to deal with difficult biting problems;
- being available to serve as an observer in a classroom struggling with ongoing biting;
- being available to help develop plans to address ongoing biting;
- monitoring progress in implementing the plan;
- acknowledging staff efforts to deal effectively with biting and congratulating staff when biting subsides;
- offering appropriate information and resources to parents regarding biting;
- being available to help staff talk with parents who are upset or frustrated.

Because biting is not unexpected, and because it can be very difficult for everyone, program administrators need to think ahead of time about how to deal with biting when it occurs. It is much easier to develop policies that make sense for children, families, and the program when you are not in the middle of the stress and frustration of an ongoing string of biting incidents. The problem is easier to address when policies have already been decided and an action plan is ready for implementation. In addition, when staff have specific training about biting, they will be more effective in preventing and responding to it. Parents who have seen a biting policy in enrollment materials or in a parent handbook also are better prepared when biting occurs. All of this means that when you have policies in place before an outbreak of biting, the biting episode is likely to be less stressful for everyone involved. It will probably be less severe, end sooner, produce less friction between parents and staff, and thus be much easier on the program and the children.

Biting and plans to deal with it are important areas for staff development in toddler programs. Topics should include

- Describing the program's philosophy and how it guides the program's policy on biting
- Reviewing toddler development
- Understanding the many different reasons toddlers bite
- Examining how the classroom environment affects biting
- Responding appropriately and effectively to biting

- Documenting biting incidents
- Observing toddlers
- Creating plans to address biting based on observations
- Talking with parents about biting

Staff development seminars give toddler caregivers the opportunity to consider and discuss their feelings about biting. The behaviors we use with children come from our attitudes, beliefs, and perceptions. If we are having trouble implementing (or even imagining) appropriate responses to biting, we may need to start by working on our attitudes, beliefs, and perceptions.

Administrators also need to prepare parents for the possibility of biting. This is a little more difficult than preparing staff, because you can hardly send parents a letter telling them to expect their child to be bitten in your program. What you *can* do is incorporate biting information in a memo or handbook that welcomes parents who are new to the toddler program. This memo or handbook should contain information on many aspects of the program, such as activities, schedule, staff, and so on. The information you provide on biting should focus on the specific steps your program takes when biting occurs. Specifics become very important to parents when their child has been bitten. The steps should, of course, reflect the decisions and plans you made as a staff. Developing this biting information for parents is important because it makes you review the steps you take and consider how these steps would sound to parents. Although we urge you to develop an information sheet that reflects your own decisions and plans concerning biting, a sample letter is offered in appendix A to help you get started.

Developing Policies about Biting

It is certainly tempting to wonder whether it's really necessary to have formal policies about biting in child care programs. The problem with not having policies is that when biting occurs, we do not have a position from which to address it. We are operating in a default mode: we haven't really thought about the issue or come to any understanding about it. When we are faced with a situation related to the issue, we end up doing whatever occurs to us at the moment. Our actions, then, are likely to be very inconsistent. In addition, if someone exerts pressure on us one way or the other, our actions are much more likely to go in the direction of that pressure. This is not a very comfortable position to be in, and certainly not a very professional one. It does a disservice to the children, families, and staff in the program.

Some programs have a policy that simply states they will deal with biting on a case-by-case basis. This is really a nonpolicy, because the programs are not taking, planning to take, or able to take any actions until after biting has happened. While in some situations we truly can't take any action until after something occurs, we can reasonably anticipate biting and can therefore plan our response to it. We can expect it will be potentially quite emotionally charged and the way we deal with it will be very involved. A nonpolicy does not prepare us for any of this. Consider this analogy from another profession:

> *Firefighters certainly have to wait until there's a fire before they can react to it. However, they don't wait around until there's a fire to begin planning how they will fight it. They take a proactive stance and prepare for reacting to fires: they order equipment, participate in training, practice, develop policies and procedures, test their equipment, and much more.*

We don't have to operate from a default mode. We can choose instead to operate from a decisive mode. This means we have given thought to an issue and have come to some understanding about it. This becomes our perspective. We then use that perspective to make a conscious decision about how we will approach situations related to the issue. These are our policies—the foundations on which our practices are built. Practices based on well thought-out decisions are much more likely to be appropriate for children, families, and staff—including ourselves. However, we can't make good decisions without that foundation.

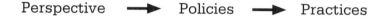

Perspective ➡ Policies ➡ Practices

Policy Components

Written policies that are clear and well thought-out help ensure that biting will be dealt with appropriately and consistently by staff. These policies can also serve as a basis for discussing parents' concerns and suggestions. If a single agency or owner operates several early childhood programs, one policy should be used consistently in all the programs. Include the following in your policies on biting:

An introduction stating the program's perspective on biting. The way the program views biting sets the stage for everything else it does related to biting. Program staff who take the time to think carefully about biting are likely to develop, choose, and implement effective strategies to address it successfully.

How staff respond to biting. Your policy should state how staff will respond to individual biting incidents as well as to episodes of ongoing biting. You may choose to use a general statement, such as "Our staff express strong disapproval of biting. They work to keep the children safe and help the child who bit learn different, more appropriate behavior. When we have episodes of ongoing biting, we develop a plan of specific strategies, techniques, and timelines to address it. This plan is shared with all parents in the group." This part of the policy may also include specific actions that are prohibited when responding to biting. For example, you may want to add a sentence such as this: "Because we want the biting to stop as quickly as possible, we don't use techniques that alarm, hurt, or frighten children, such as biting back or washing a child's mouth out with soap."

How parents are informed about biting. Your policy should detail the procedure for informing parents about biting, including any special procedure for the parents of the child who bit and the parents of the child who was bitten. It should also include procedures for informing all parents when there is ongoing biting serious enough to warrant an action plan in the program.

How biting is documented. Your program should require that all incidents of biting be documented using the program's standard incident report forms. Make sure all staff are familiar with completing these forms, making them available to parents, and filing a copy with the program administration. If your program does not have such forms, see the examples in appendix C.

The role of confidentiality. Your policy should include what information concerning biting is kept confidential. Most often, this applies to the name of the child who bit or is biting. The reason for this confidentiality is that we do not want children labeled on the basis of only one of their behaviors. As discussed earlier, it is unfortunately very common to hear a child called "a biter." Remember that being labeled "a biter" defines the child in a negative way and makes it more difficult to work quickly and positively toward stopping the biting. In addition, parents may take it on themselves to chastise the child who bit their child or to try to punish that child's parents. Confidentiality is a cornerstone of professionalism in the early childhood field. You cannot practice selective confidentiality and still expect to build trusting relationships with parents.

What first aid is given for biting. First aid for biting should be based on medical advice and an understanding of the risk of infection. You can use the information on pages 19–20 to develop and communicate your own policies.

A sample policy for you to refer to when developing your own policy can be found in appendix A.

What about a "Three Bites and You're Out" Policy?

Some directors, staff, and parents want to have a policy that expels children from the program after a certain number of bites. This seems logical and fair to many adults. The idea is similar to the "three strikes and you're out" laws currently in effect around the country. This approach has many problems as a policy to address biting.

What underlies such a policy is a belief that toddlers are solely responsible every time they bite and that they can make conscious, informed decisions not to bite. We know, however, that many factors can contribute to biting, and not all of them are within the child's control. The environment, for example, is the caregivers' responsibility. If the biting were the direct result of an inappropriate environment, would anyone suggest there be a "three bites and you don't have to pay for a week of child care" policy or a "three bites and the teacher gets fired" policy?

The goal of this kind of exclusion policy is not to help the toddler learn different, more appropriate behavior but to eliminate children from the program when they don't behave in acceptable ways. The problem is that all toddlers behave in unacceptable ways some of the time—that's part of how they learn how to do what is acceptable. Like all learning, this is a slow, two-steps-forward-one-step-back process. When you have a policy like "three bites and you're out," caregivers no longer focus on helping toddlers but rather on counting bites. It puts caregivers in a terrible position, because this policy is "legalistic" in nature, and legalistic approaches create legalistic complications.

For example, what should actually "count" as a bite? Caregivers may have an eagle eye out for the third bite from a child who is difficult to work with. As soon as teeth are bared, the third bite is recorded, and the child has to leave because "that's our policy." For a child who is in better graces, adults may decide not to count a bite that "wasn't really a bite; it was just a little nip." Sometimes biting happens, and no one sees it. Must a child be "charged" with the bite? And isn't it likely that a child who has been biting will be the chief suspect?

Caregivers and parents may also decide that there is such a thing as "a justified bite." If a child bites because another child hit him, should that bite count?

What happens when there is a discrepancy in the bite count? A teacher or caregiver may insist a child has reached the magic number of bites, but a parent is sure the child still has one more to go.

Furthermore, what is the time frame for counting these bites? Three bites in a day? Three bites in a week? Three bites in a month? Is there a statute of limitations so if a child doesn't bite for two months, his previous bite record is erased, and he starts over? Does the bite count go with him to the next toddler room?

We know about half of children bite during the toddler years. A "three bites and you're out" policy might create a contingent of "wandering toddlers" who go from one program to another in which the same thing could happen. Instead of responsive, consistent care, the toddler might endure a series of short-term child care experiences. This, of course, would put more stress on the child, increasing the chance that he would bite, while limiting the opportunity for him to learn from stable, loving caregivers how to behave differently.

Toddlers might not be the only victims of this policy. It could also hurt the program it was designed to protect. Enrollment could suffer because parents who must take their toddler out of a program would most likely take older siblings out too. Moreover, teachers would not be working on developing the skills and creating the environments that effectively address biting. These skills and environments enhance the overall quality of the program and benefit all the children, not just those who are biting.

Biting as a Reason to Exclude Children

Should biting be a reason to exclude a child from your program? This is a touchy subject because it is a frequent request, demand, or even ultimatum from parents. Anyone who has been a director for any length of time has heard something to the effect of "Either you kick that biter out, or I'm pulling my child out of here." When faced with such an ultimatum, it is certainly tempting to solve the problem by expelling the child who is biting. This may be especially true when you risk losing several families. It may seem like a simple solution to a complicated problem.

It is not, however, a simple solution. Let's consider the program implications first. A program that expels a child for biting is indicating either that it doesn't know enough to work on the problem or that it is unwilling to work on the problem—or both! A program that considers itself lacking the knowledge, skill, and motivation to deal with biting is most likely going to lack knowledge, skill, and motivation in its work with children. Is this what we are offering parents and children? When we do the hard work of acquiring knowledge, developing skills, and providing the best for children, our programs become stronger and more appropriate for children and families. When we excuse ourselves from doing this, our programs become weaker. Programs that have actively, painfully, and successfully addressed biting do not use biting as a reason to exclude children. And they often lose very few families as a result of their policies.

Let's also consider the child who is biting and her family. When a child is biting repeatedly, she needs help to learn other, more appropriate behavior from adults she knows and trusts. This is the most likely way to stop the biting. But it can't happen if she goes from program to program, from adults she knows and trusts to adults who are strangers. Parents may feel they must either avoid or lie about the reason for leaving the previous program when they try to enroll their child in a new one. As a result, they can't get the help and support they need.

Programs often claim to be justified in expelling a child for biting because they have "tried everything." When programs call Child Care Solutions with this statement, it usually turns out that "everything" has been a short list of approaches—some appropriate and some not—tried once or twice each. We urge programs to try the approaches in this book consistently for several weeks. While this will require more effort, that effort is likely to pay off.

Sometimes a Child Should Leave the Program

As committed as most caregivers are to the children and families in their programs, a few children do need a different kind of setting to stop biting. This is determined after trying all other approaches consistently over time. Most likely, biting is not the only problem the child is having in the program. In such a case, your program should review what it has tried and perhaps ask for outside help in this review. If you conclude that the needs of the child are beyond what even a good program—one with knowledge, skill, and motivation—can provide, you must face the possibility that this child might need a different kind of setting or program. Sometimes, for example, a very sensitive child is too overwhelmed by a large infant/toddler program and really needs the smaller group size and multiage character of a good family child care home. This admission comes with regret. When this happens, you need to provide support to the child's parents. Make sure you know how to refer the parent to other resources to find appropriate care for their child. You can start with your local child care resource and referral agency.

Biting and HIV/AIDS

Parents and caregivers may express concern over transmission of HIV/AIDS through biting and may even cite it as a reason to exclude a child who is biting. The Task Force on Biting contacted AIDS Community Resources, our local source for information on HIV/AIDS. At the time, that organization provided us with information indicating that HIV/AIDS was not transmitted through biting. The information was based on a 1994 statement by a spokesperson for the federal Centers for Disease Control and Prevention (CDC).

Since then, the CDC has provided us with additional information about this issue. According to the CDC Web site (updated in October 2006), an incident reported in 1997 suggested blood-to-blood transmission of HIV through biting. There are also "rare reports in the medical literature in which HIV appeared to have been transmitted by a bite." In each of these incidents, the CDC reports that there was "severe trauma with extensive tissue tearing and damage and presence of blood." These were not noted as incidents of *children* biting. The CDC states that "biting is not a common way of transmitting HIV."

Blood-to-blood contact through biting would be very unusual among toddlers, and parents are often more worried about saliva. The CDC reports that contact with saliva "has never been shown to result in transmission of HIV."

AIDS Community Resources urges child care programs and providers to get their information on HIV/AIDS from a reliable source and suggests that they call the CDC National AIDS Hotline at 800-342-2437. There is also a Spanish language hotline at 800-344-7432 and a TTY line at 800-243-7889.

Documenting Biting

All bites should be documented on the forms your program uses for incidents. Using these forms for biting is an indication to parents that your program takes biting seriously and that you are not trying to hide biting incidents. Incident forms also help address the problem that arises when the teacher who is with the child at pickup time is not the teacher who was in the program when the bite occurred. These forms may also be useful when looking at biting patterns, because they contain specific information about time, place, and circumstances of the biting.

Because biting understandably stirs strong emotions in parents, an incident form left in the child's cubby for the parent to discover may be seen as uncaring. You need to tell parents face-to-face about the biting. Your words, tone, and body language should convey genuine regret that their child was bitten. Giving parents this news is not easy, and parents consistently tell us they want caregivers to be as upset about the bite as they are and to take it as seriously as they do. After parents have had the chance to make sure their child is all right, you can give them the incident form.

Most programs have their own incident forms already in place. We have included three sample forms in appendix C if you need a template or want to revise the form your program currently uses. If you have a choice, we suggest using an incident report instead of an accident report. Reporting the bite as an "accident" may be inflammatory to parents who insist "This was no accident. It was deliberate!"

Appendix A

Sample Letters for Parents and Policy Statements
for Staff and Parents

Letter Informing Parents of Plans to Address Ongoing Biting

Dear Parents,

As you know, we have been struggling with biting in our toddler room. We are all worried about it, and we know you are frustrated by it. When biting becomes an ongoing problem, our policy is to develop a plan to address it based on observation of the children and our program. We have just completed our plan and want to share it with you.

First, we noticed that most of the biting was taking place when children were crowded in the block area. Second, we noticed that the biting usually started when a child bit out of frustration, and other children responded by biting. Third, when we checked our program, we had to admit that we were not providing many sensory activities, which usually serve to calm and soothe children. Fourth, we noticed there were never any biting incidents when we went outside.

We used these observations to develop the following plan:

1. We have made two block areas in the room so children will not be bunched up in one block area. These areas are on opposite ends of the room. We're not sure we'll keep it this way, but we want to try it for now.
2. We are stepping up our language development activities with children who are still learning to use words to express their frustration.
3. We have added some sensory activities and materials to the program. We have set up water play in little basins on the table. We have also added some squares of velour material (Thank you, Mrs. Jackson, for this donation) to our dress-up area.
4. We are going to go outside one more time per day to increase the amount of time when there is no biting so children become used to a daily routine without biting.

We'll be trying these strategies for the next two weeks. During that time we'll keep track of the biting to see if it decreases. Please bear with us. We know that positive actions work much better than negative ones, and we're doing our best to provide them.

We know this has not been a pleasant time for you, and we appreciate your support while we work to stop this biting. If you have any questions, please let us know.

—Carmen Espinoza, Teacher
—Nancy Jones, Teacher
—LaTanya Roberts, Director

Letter Informing Parents of How the Program Approaches Biting

Dear Parents,

We are always upset when we experience biting in our toddler rooms. Even though we know biting is not entirely unexpected when toddlers are together in groups, we don't want any of your children to be bitten, and we want any child who bites to learn more appropriate behavior. When it comes to biting, here is what you can expect from us:

- We will put children's safety first and provide appropriate first aid as well as comfort, support, and advice to any child who is bitten.
- We will provide appropriate programming for toddlers to help prevent biting.
- We will make current information and resources on biting available for you.
- We will provide teachers with adequate knowledge and training to deal appropriately and effectively with biting.
- We will take your concerns seriously and treat them with understanding and respect.
- We will tell you what specific steps we are taking to address biting and explain the reasoning behind those steps.
- We will respond to your questions, concerns, and suggestions—even when our response to some suggestions is no.
- We will work to schedule conferences about biting with your child's teachers at a time when you can attend.
- We will keep your child's identity confidential if he or she bites. This helps avoid labeling or confrontations that will slow the process of learning not to bite.

Please don't hesitate to come to any of us with questions or concerns.

Sincerely,

    —Kirsten Petersen
    —Johnetta Carmichael
    —Cindy Chang

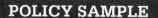
POLICY SAMPLE

Sample Content on Biting for Parent Handbook

Along with all the other information we have given you about our toddler room, we want you to know about our response to biting. Biting is unfortunately not unexpected in toddler groups but can be very emotionally charged. There are many reasons toddlers may bite. Sometimes the biting is related to teething. Sometimes toddlers bite to express feelings they can't express with words yet. We have seen children bite when they are frustrated, and we have seen them bite in the excitement of a happy moment. No one can predict which children will bite, but we are ready to help toddlers who do bite to learn other behavior. We are also ready to give treatment, sympathy, and advice to children who are bitten. Here are the ways we work to prevent biting and how we respond to it when it does happen.

First, we try to program the day to avoid boredom, frustration, or overstimulation. We provide a calm and cheerful atmosphere with a mix of stimulating, soothing, age-appropriate activities and multiples of favorite toys. We also work to model acceptable and appropriate behaviors for the children, helping them learn words to express their feelings and giving them tools to resolve conflicts with our help.

Second, if a bite does occur, we help the child who was bitten. We reassure him or her and care for the bite. If the skin is not broken, we use a cold pack. If the skin is broken, we follow medical advice and clean the bite with soap and water. If it is likely the bite may get dirty, we will cover it to keep it clean. If your child is bitten, we will call you to let you know about the bite. The teachers fill out an incident report, have it signed by our administrators, keep a copy, and give one to you when you pick up your child. We also respond to the child who did the biting. We show the children strong disapproval of biting. Our specific response varies by circumstances, but our basic message is that biting is the wrong thing to do. We also help the child who bit learn different, more appropriate behavior, and we let his or her parents know there's a problem so we can work together to solve it.

Third, the teachers and administration analyze the cause of ongoing biting. We develop a plan to address the causes of the biting, focusing on keeping children safe and helping those who are stuck in biting patterns. When we need to develop such a plan, we share the details with parents so they know specifically how we are addressing this problem.

Fourth, parents are notified if their child starts to bite. We ask parents to keep us informed if their child is biting at home. Children who bite in our program do not necessarily bite at home. But if your child is biting in both places, it is important for all of us to be consistent in dealing with it. Communication is very important in order to help your child stop biting.

We wish we could guarantee that biting will never happen in our program, but we know there is no such guarantee. You can count on us to deal appropriately with biting so it will end as quickly as possible. We will support your children whether they bite or are bitten. We want the best for all the children in our program. If you want more information on biting or have any questions or concerns, please let us know.

Biting Policy

Our program recognizes that biting is unfortunately not unexpected when toddlers are in group care. We are always upset when children are bitten in our program, and we recognize how upsetting biting is for parents. While we feel that biting is never the right thing for toddlers to do, we know that they bite for a variety of reasons. Most of these reasons are not related to behavior problems. Our program does not focus on punishment for biting but on effective techniques that address the specific reason for the biting. When biting occurs, these are our three main responses:

1. Care and help for the child who was bitten.
2. Help for the child who bit so that he or she learns other behavior.
3. Examination of our program to stop the biting.

Our teachers express strong disapproval of biting. They work to keep children safe and to help the child who bit learn different, more appropriate behavior. When there are episodes of ongoing biting, we develop a plan of specific strategies, techniques, and timelines to address it. We do not use any response that harms a child or is known to be ineffective.

We give immediate attention and, if necessary, first aid to children who are bitten. We offer to put ice on the bite if the child is willing. If the skin is broken, we clean the wound with soap and water. If children are bitten on the top of their hands and the skin is broken, we recommend they be seen by their health care provider.

When children bite, their parents are informed personally and privately the same day. When children are bitten, their parents are informed personally and given a copy of our incident form. When we experience ongoing biting in a toddler room, we share the written plan we have developed with all parents of children in the room.

Biting is always documented on our standard incident report form, which is completed and signed by a teacher and an administrator. It must also be signed by the parent. One copy is given to the parents, and the other copy is kept in the incident report book in the office.

We keep the name of the child who bit confidential. This is to avoid labeling and to give our teachers the opportunity to use their time and energy to work on stopping the biting.

Once a year, toddler caregivers attend a training session on biting. In addition, we have current resources on biting available for staff and parents. We encourage parents to bring their concerns and frustrations directly to the teachers.

Appendix B
Sample Observations

Two examples of the kinds of observations that are useful to help us craft effective plans for reducing biting are included here. These are adaptations of actual observations and the resulting recommendations. I observed the children during the course of working with teachers and used staff observations, reflections, and insights to understand the children and the settings. The resulting recommendations do not call for additional staff or for teachers to drastically alter what they do in their programs. All the recommendations can be accomplished by caring teachers in busy toddler programs.

The names of the children, the teachers, the rooms, and the centers have been changed. The observations and recommendations were made available to parents as well as teachers.

Jeffrey P., age 26 months, and the Rainbow Room

LMNOP Child Care Center

Gretchen Kinnell, Director of Education and Training, Child Care Solutions

I had visited the Rainbow Room earlier in the month, but I came to observe Jeffrey on September 28. The observation lasted from 8:30 to 10:05 AM. There were nine children present, ranging from 24 months to 32 months. Melissa, the head teacher, was in the room the entire time. Annie, the assistant teacher, arrived at 9:00. From 8:30 to 9:00 there was another staff person in the room who left when Annie arrived. During the time I was there, the children engaged in free play, had snack, and prepared to go outdoors.

On this visit, I noticed that the teachers were more directly involved with the children, spending more time with them one-on-one and in small groups. (During the earlier observation the teachers were more involved with tasks in the room.) The teachers were responsive to the children as individuals and geared their interactions to the personalities and needs of each child. They also showed a genuine appreciation of and delight in each child. All the children were actively and happily engaged in activities, and there were few conflicts. This level of responsiveness and interaction will be essential in working with Jeffrey to stop the biting.

During free play, Jeffrey was very focused on his own activities. The teachers and children genuinely like him and were willing to interact with him, but he acknowledged and warmed up to other people slowly. Jeffrey played quietly by himself during most of the first forty-five minutes I observed. Although he did not play with other children (typical of toddler play), he was in close proximity to them, and none of them moved away from or avoided him. He was very focused on the toys he was playing with, and at first barely acknowledged Melissa when she talked to him. He averted his gaze and kept playing with his toys. He did the same thing when another little boy came over and said, "Hi." At one point Jeffrey got his hand stuck in a toy. He cried softly, and Melissa came over to help him. He recovered very quickly.

As the morning progressed, Jeffrey began to interact more with Melissa. He sat in her lap and was quite relaxed as he smiled and listened to her. He also looked at what other children were doing and occasionally walked over near them. At 9:15, after a relaxed and uneventful period of free play, Jeffrey went to a little girl who had another train he wanted. He tried to take it from her with no words and no warning. She protested very loudly and held on to it tightly. He responded by trying to hit her and by crying loudly. His crying and attempts to hit her increased. At that point, his teacher and I both went up to him. I was the first person to reach him; I took him in my arms, rubbed his back, and used a quiet, soothing tone of voice to say, "It's so hard when you can't have what you want. I know. It's hard." He calmed down very quickly and then was easily redirected by his teacher to something else. At 9:25 there was another incident that was almost identical. It was a different child and a different toy, but Jeffrey quickly began to cry and tried to hit. His teacher handled the situation much the same way I had in the earlier incident. At 9:28 there was a third incident that was again identical to the first two. Melissa said that this was typical of the situations that had led to his biting in the past.

Immediately after the 9:28 incident, it was time for snack. Jeffrey was the first person to seat himself at the table. He buckled himself in and played with a toy by himself quite contentedly until the rest of the children were seated. He did not interact with the other children during snack. He yawned and had second helpings, and he was the last child to leave the snack table— by his own choice. We know that toddlers often bite when they are physically tired, hungry, or overwhelmed. Perhaps snack time was an opportunity for Jeffrey to regroup.

From observing Jeffrey and talking with Melissa, several patterns emerged that will form the basis for the plan to help him learn to stop biting. First was that when Jeffrey played by himself, he did quite well, but when he initiated contact with other children it was often to get something he wanted. He didn't use language but just tried to take the object.

Second, he wasn't able to manage his emotional response to the situation when he met resistance. I want to note that this is in no way a deficiency; it is quite typical of toddlers. Left on his own, he became more and more emotionally distraught. However, he responded very positively and very quickly to being comforted and soothed by an adult. This is a very good sign because self-control develops from external to internal. He responded very well to external help and did not fight it. It was also evident from the timeline of the incidents that once he began to have trouble dealing with his emotions, it escalated. In the last incident, the little girl decided to give Jeffrey the toy. The teachers said this little girl is quite aware of other children's feelings, and she gave him the toy willingly. He accepted the toy, played with it for a minute or so, and then gave it back to her and said, "Thank you." He knows what to do, and when he is not emotionally bound up, he can do it. But when he is struggling with strong emotions, he cannot regain control by himself.

Third, from the toys he selected and the way he played with them, it was evident that Jeffrey has very good small motor skills for his age. He was very focused in his small-motor play. He is one of the youngest children in the room, but he hitched the cars of a toy train together and could easily buckle the little seat belts on the chairs. Two other children tried to hitch the train cars but could not do it. They could see how the cars should go together but did not have the fine-motor skills to do it. Melissa reported that of the ten children in the room, only three can fasten the seat belts, and Jeffrey is one of them. Jeffrey was also very persistent when working on various tasks with toys. He put a helmet on and spent two minutes turning and turning it until it fit just right.

It is possible that Jeffrey's persistence may play a role in his biting. Melissa said that even though Jeffrey often bit when he had conflicts with other children over toys, he sometimes bit after the conflict was over. He would walk away seemingly composed and then bite someone else, sometimes even later. It seems that Jeffrey also may be persistent in his need to express his frustration.

Plan to Help Reduce Jeffrey's Biting

First, the teachers should continue giving Jeffrey the positive attention and gentle physical interactions he enjoys. They should continue to support his play when he is playing alone and at the same time point out what other children around him are doing. This will help him become more aware of others. Second, even more effective than having one person shadowing him is having the teachers who interact with him most watch for situations in which he may not be able to manage his emotions. When that happens, the first step should be to move in, move him away from the other child (or move the other child away from him), and help him calm down with circular motions or gentle pats on the back, a soothing tone of voice, and words that acknowledge how hard it is for him. When he does calm down, he needs to be told that the other child is playing with the toy now and that he can play with something else. This should be followed by redirecting him to a different toy and by reinforcing his calming down with a short comment like, "Good for you. Now you're fine and playing with a ball." The teachers did a very good job of this on the day I observed. They knew exactly what kind of toy to redirect him to. This approach will provide the external control he needs at this point, which will be the foundation on which he can develop internal control.

The teachers should also help Jeffrey learn new social skills by watching for times when he wants a toy another child has. If they can intervene before he begins getting upset, they can tell him, "You're looking at the train. Jackie has it now. Ask Jackie, 'Please?' Maybe you can play with it." Then, of course, give Jackie the option of saying yes or no. If she says no, the teachers should say matter-of-factly, "Jackie still wants to play with it." Redirect him to something else. Little by little the teachers can help him learn more and more of the language of asking for something. He has already shown that he is able to apply this kind of social skill when he is not emotionally embroiled.

The teachers can also help him develop competence at interacting with other children by playing with Jeffrey for a minute or so with a toy designed to go back and forth between two people—like a ball. Then the teacher can invite another child to come over and play too. The teachers should choose a child who is likely to agree to do this. The teacher should then stay close to Jeffrey to support him as he plays with the other child. This does not have to last long. It will give Jeffrey some supported and successful interactions with other children.

We also want to capitalize on Jeffrey's interest, fine-motor skills, and persistence. He has already mastered the fine-motor toys in the room. Let's try bringing in toys that require more advanced fine-motor skills from other classrooms. At first you'll probably need to bring in duplicates of the toys because, being new, the toys will interest other children and they will want to explore them too. This will give Jeffrey the opportunity to feel the satisfaction that comes with doing something he enjoys and is good at.

Finally, the teachers must be aware of Jeffrey's physical needs. He had more trouble managing his emotions when he was hungry and tired and after he had already had other emotional episodes. He recovered after having his snack and having time when he did not interact with other children. Teachers might schedule short one-on-one lap times with Jeffrey at around 9:15—just before snack—to give him the physical support that seems to help him emotionally. Teachers should also point out to him when he has used language to thank someone for sharing or to ask for something. This will be his clue that these are the behaviors to continue.

Matthew R., age 21 months, and the Sunshine Room

XYZ Child Care Center

Gretchen Kinnell, Director of Education and Training, Child Care Solutions

I observed Matthew in his classroom on October 26 from 9:00 to 10:30 AM. There were four children in the room during the observation, ages 17 through 25 months. Amber, the teacher, was there the entire time. Candace, another teacher, arrived at 9:10 and was there for the remainder of the time. While I was there, the children engaged in free play, had snack, and played in the gross-motor room. The teachers also changed diapers as necessary.

I observed four types of behavior that I think relate to Matthew's biting and will be keys to developing an approach to help him learn to stop biting.

First, he has a great deal of oral-motor activity—he puts everything in his mouth. He also enjoys manipulating his mouth to make sounds. During the observation, he

- sucked his thumb while Candace read to him;
- put Elmo's big plastic eyes in his mouth so that the rest of Elmo was hanging out of his mouth;
- specifically sought the smaller balls in the gross-motor area so that he could get his mouth on them more easily;
- put small toys—cars and a toy ambulance—in his mouth;
- made "raspberry" sounds and seemed quite delighted with himself;
- exchanged a big, round ball for a football after he couldn't get his mouth on the round ball very well. As soon as he had the football, he put the end in his mouth and smiled;
- sought out and enthusiastically used musical instruments that work by blowing into them;
- kept a small ball in his mouth even when trying to climb up a step in the gross-motor room;
- had his mouth wide open much of the time, whether he was smiling broadly or crying.

Second, I observed that Matthew sought out contact with other adults and children. He readily ran up to me when I came into the room, even though he had never seen me before. He enjoyed physical attention with his teachers, sitting in Candace's lap as she read him a book and hugging both Candace and Amber often. As is typical of toddlers, Matthew played near other children but not with them. He handed them toys and kept one eye on what they were doing. On one occasion he hit Liam when Liam got too close to him. Candace and Amber often redirected children—including Matthew—when they got very close together and began to tussle over toys.

Third, I observed that Matthew had rapidly developing language abilities and he delighted in his own speech. During my stay he pointed at toys and, making sure I was paying attention, announced, "Ball!" "Kitty!" "Dog!" He was very engrossed in a story Candace read with him one-on-one. He pointed to a picture of a boy in the book and told Candace quite insistently, "Mack!" Candace then told me that Matthew has an older brother, Max, who looks a bit like the boy in the picture. At snacktime, Candace and Amber were talking with the children about their families, and Matthew pointed to Candace and then looked at me and said, "Mack bus." His speech was not completely clear, but within a very short time, Candace and I understood what he was saying. Not only was Matthew telling me (correctly, as it turned out) that Max was on the bus, but by pointing to Candace he was indicating that he knew Candace had put Max on the bus. This type of sentence, called a "telegraphic sentence" because it only includes the key words, is one of the milestones in language development for toddlers.

Finally, I saw Matthew try to get into small, semiprivate spaces several times. He tried about three times to go into the space behind the classroom door, which was open. He also climbed into the bottom shelf of the bookshelf, which was just a few inches above the floor.

Plan to Reduce Matthew's Biting

While Matthew did not bite during the morning I observed him, we can use these observations to look at why he might be biting and to formulate a plan to help him stop. First, a great deal of toddler biting is related to oral-motor exploration, and Matthew exhibited a constant need for oral-motor involvement. To help address this need and reduce the likelihood of biting, physical and occupational therapists recommend that children be allowed opportunities to explore with their mouths. Here are several suggestions:

- Allow him to put things in his mouth as long as they are safe. (Set aside items he has mouthed for later disinfecting. You can disinfect toys by washing and spraying them with a solution of one part bleach to ten parts water solution and allowing the toys to air dry. This would be true for toys all children mouth, not just those that Matthew mouths.)
- Give him oral-motor activities on a daily basis—blowing bubbles is a good one.
- Have him play musical instruments that require blowing to make sound.
- Have him blow pinwheels to make them go around and around.

- Have him blow on crepe paper streamers to make them move.
- Have him blow on wind chimes to make sounds.

Second, Matthew does not know what to do with other toddlers when they get too close to him or when they do things he doesn't like. This is often a reason toddlers bite. Amber and Candace should continue watching toddlers who are interacting, notice when conflicts start to develop, and then redirect the children away from each other.

Third, they can begin putting language with situations. Many toddlers bite when they do not have language to express themselves, so I suggest capitalizing on Matthew's exploding language acquisition by engaging in conversations with him, verbally describing situations, and putting words to actions and things. An example would be, "Oh, dear. Liam has the ball, and Matthew wants it. Liam is playing with it now. Let's find another ball for Matthew." This gives Matthew an explanation of what is going on and guides him toward a solution that does not involve biting (or hitting, for that matter). And the more competence he has with language, the more likely it is that he will not bite.

Finally, since Matthew sought and enjoyed being in small, private spaces, the teachers should create some. It might be a large cardboard box that has a door and is open on the top (and anchored by a pillow) so he can be by himself and still be under their supervision. They will probably have to make more than one of these, since other children will also love them.

Appendix C

Incident Report Samples

Incident Report

Sample 1

Child's Name _____ Child's Age _____

Date of Incident ____ / ____ / ____ Time of Incident _____ AM PM

How was the child injured? What was child doing when hurt? _____

_____

_____

Were there other children or adults involved? How? _____

_____

_____

Location and description of the injury _____

_____

_____

Was any care given on-site? YES NO If yes, describe _____

_____

_____

Was the child's parent/guardian notified? (Circle one) YES NO

Was a physician contacted? YES NO By whom? _____

When? _____ Physician's Name _____

Describe any advice given by the physician on the back of this report.

Recommendation for future injury prevention _____

_____

_____

_____

Signature of Staff Member _____ Date _____

Signature of Additional Witness _____ Date _____

Signature of Director _____ Date _____

Signature of Parent _____ Date _____

❐ ORIGINAL COPY—OFFICE   ❐ COPY—PARENT/GUARDIAN   ❐ COPY—CHILD'S FOLDER

Incident Report

Sample 2

Child's Name _____ Child's Age _____

Date of Incident _____ / _____ / _____ Type _____
(accident, illness, etc.)

Time of Incident _____ AM   PM   Place _____
(playground, name of classroom, etc.)

Describe the incident _____

_____

_____

Describe the injuries _____

_____

_____

Describe first aid or other attention provided _____

_____

_____

_____

Parent / Guardian Notified _____

Signature of Parent _____
Date   Time   AM   PM

Signature of Staff Completing Report _____

Signature of Witness _____

Incident Report

Sample 3

Child's Name_____ Date ____ / ____ / ____ Time_____ AM PM

Cause and description of injury or incident_____

_____

_____

_____

_____

Action taken / First aid given _____

_____

_____

Additional comments / Follow-up _____

_____

_____

_____

Staff Signature_____ Date Report Completed_____

Parent / Guardian Signature _____ Date _____

Text © 2008 by Child Care Solutions, Inc. Published by Redleaf Press (www.redleafpress.org).
May be reproduced for use in a child care program or staff training.